LUKE]
BIOGRAPHY

A British Maestro At The Heart Of Global Golf

Michael D. Grimsley

All rights reserved. No part of this publication may be reproduced, distributed, or transmitted in any form or by any means, including photocopying, recording, or other electronic or mechanical method, without the prior written permission of the publisher, except in the case of brief quotations embodied in critical reviews and certain other noncommercial uses permitted by the copyright law.

Copyright © **Michael D. Grimsley**, 2025.

DISCLAIMER

This book is an independent, unofficial biography. It is not authorized, endorsed, licensed, or approved by the individual, their family, representatives, or affiliated entities.

All information contained in this publication is based on publicly available sources, journalistic research, and personal interpretation. The author and publisher have made every effort to ensure factual accuracy and fair representation at the time of publication.

This work is intended for educational and informational purposes only. Names, trademarks, and images that may appear in this book are the property of their respective owners and are used in a descriptive and editorial context only.

If any individual or organization believes this book infringes upon their rights, they are encouraged to contact the publisher directly for immediate review and resolution.

Table of Contents

Introduction 5

Chapter 1: Roots of a Champion 13

Chapter 2: Swinging into Promise 28

Chapter 3: Across the Atlantic 43

Chapter 4: Turning Pro and Taking Aim 58

Chapter 5: Climbing the World Rankings 75

Chapter 6: Rivalries, Respect, and the Ryder Cup. 91

Chapter 7: The Art of the Game 107

Chapter 8: Challenges, Injuries, and Comebacks. 124

Chapter 9: Captaincy and Legacy 140

Chapter 10: Beyond the Fairways 154

Conclusion 169

INTRODUCTION

Every so often, sport produces a figure who transcends statistics, who redefines what excellence looks like without needing to raise their voice or chase spectacle. Luke Donald belongs to that rare category. His name doesn't conjure the image of booming drives or flamboyant celebrations. Instead, it evokes precision, calm authority, and an artistry that feels almost orchestral. To watch him play was to see balance in motion, a man whose every swing carried thought, patience, and a quiet command that set him apart from the chaos of modern competition.

Golf has never lacked for personalities, yet Luke carved out a space uniquely his own. Where others pursued raw power, he elevated finesse. Where flash often drew the spotlight, he earned admiration through restraint. His story isn't one of sudden ascension or overnight triumph but of thoughtful construction, a life shaped by discipline, patience, and a near-obsessive dedication to the craft. The journey from the suburbs of England to the pinnacle of the world rankings tells more than a story about sport; it reflects a philosophy about how success, when pursued with humility and intelligence, can endure far beyond the fairways.

From his earliest days with a club in hand, there was an unmistakable poise about Luke. He didn't look like the kind of player who would overpower a course, yet his confidence was undeniable. Those who watched him as a teenager saw a competitor whose strength lay not in volume but in detail. His natural rhythm, combined with a sharp strategic mind, made him stand out even before his name appeared in headlines. He learned to win not by forcing outcomes but by understanding them by reading conditions, studying tendencies, and trusting the quiet repetition that turns talent into mastery.

That approach became the foundation of his career and his identity.

This book delves into that evolution from the driven young golfer seeking belonging on foreign courses to the composed professional who defined a generation's understanding of precision. It's a chronicle not just of tournaments and trophies, but of temperament, transformation, and thought. Luke Donald's path was never purely about conquering the leaderboard. It was about artistry, about finding the perfect note in a symphony of challenges, and about the grace it takes to keep creating when the spotlight shifts or the rhythm falters.

What makes Luke's story particularly compelling is how it challenges conventional narratives of greatness. In an era where athletes are often measured by spectacle, he showed that subtlety could be just as powerful. His rise to world number one was built not on brute force but on consistency so refined it bordered on meditative. There was elegance in his tempo, intelligence in his shot selection, and an almost painterly sense of balance in how he approached every round. He made golf look effortless, though those who knew him understood how much effort lay beneath the surface.

Beyond his technique, Luke's influence grew from his character. He was the kind of athlete who made professionalism feel personal. Every handshake, every interview, every interaction carried the same quiet respect he brought to the game itself. There was no theatrical bravado, no need for noise, only a deep appreciation for the discipline and spirit that golf demands. His demeanor reflected a timeless lesson: that greatness, when rooted in respect, outlasts trends.

Yet this isn't a tale without tension. Like every artist, Luke's mastery was tested by doubt, injury, and the relentless pressure of expectation. His journey to the summit of the sport was hard-won, and staying there demanded a kind of mental resilience that few could truly understand. What separated him wasn't just skill but composure an ability to adapt, to analyze, to stay centered even when the game threatened to unravel. His career became a case study in focus under fire, a reminder that control is as much emotional as it is technical.

There's also a deeply human quality to Luke's path. Beneath the composed exterior was a man driven by quiet ambition and shaped by moments of vulnerability. The pursuit of perfection can be isolating, and yet he managed to balance that pursuit with grace, family, and perspective. He learned to carry success lightly and to view failure not as a fracture but as a chance to refine. That mindset, patient, honest, and grounded, became his real legacy. It's what made fellow golfers admire him, what made fans root for him, and what makes his story resonate today.

This biography explores not only the chapters of his career but the nuances that made him who he is: the thoughtful student of the game, the strategist, the teammate, the leader, and the artist. It looks at the people who shaped him, the rivals who challenged him, and the choices that defined his evolution. It's a portrait of a man who found his own rhythm in a sport obsessed with power, and who built a career that reminded the world that precision could still be poetry.

Luke Donald didn't just play golf; he reinterpreted it. His presence on the course carried a kind of quiet magnetism, the kind that makes even silence feel charged. He brought back the art of control, that delicate balance between confidence and calm. Watching him was like listening to a carefully composed melody where every note, every pause, had purpose. His approach wasn't designed to dazzle; it was meant to endure. That's what made him both a champion and a craftsman.

As this book unfolds, readers will see how his story intersects with the broader evolution of modern golf, the transition from finesse to force, the rise of global competition, and the subtle shifts in what the sport values. Through all of it, Luke's consistency offered a counterpoint, a reminder that thought and elegance still had a place amid the thunder. His life and career embody a truth that reaches far beyond sport: that mastery, when built on patience and authenticity, has a resonance that time can't erase.

This is the story of a man who turned golf into art. It's about the pursuit of excellence without arrogance, the pursuit of success without spectacle. Luke Donald remains, at his core, a craftsman of moments, someone who showed the world that power isn't always loud, that the truest form of greatness lies not in domination but in balance. His journey from a young English talent to a global ambassador for the sport is one of quiet brilliance, relentless dedication, and the enduring beauty of precision.

Welcome to the world of Luke Donald where every swing tells a story, every challenge is an opportunity to refine, and every victory, no matter how understated, sings with the unmistakable rhythm of a maestro.

CHAPTER 1: ROOTS OF A CHAMPION

The story of Luke Donald begins in the quiet English town of Hemel Hempstead, Hertfordshire, where a young boy's fascination with golf took root long before the world would come to know him as one of the sport's most refined talents. Born on December 7, 1977, Luke Campbell Donald grew up in an environment that was far from the grandeur of professional golf courses. His early years were defined by modest surroundings, supportive parents, and a curiosity that found expression through a small set of clubs and the nearby local course. The son of Colin and Ann Donald, Luke was raised in a home where discipline and kindness coexisted naturally. His father worked as a managing director in the textile industry, and his mother maintained the warmth of the household that gave Luke and his older brother, Christian, the stability and encouragement they needed to explore their interests.

The Donald household valued character as much as achievement. Luke was never pushed into the sport for fame or fortune; instead, he was guided by quiet encouragement. His parents noticed early that their son possessed an unusually meticulous temperament. He was not a child of loud ambition but one of quiet determination. When he played, whether in the backyard or at the local club, he displayed a careful, methodical nature, one that would later become the defining quality of his professional career. Every swing, every adjustment, every motion mattered. There was something artistic about the way he treated the game, even as a child. He sought not only to play well but to play beautifully, with grace and balance.

Golf entered his life through his father's gentle interest in the game. Colin often took his sons to practice at local clubs, and Luke quickly became fascinated by the challenge. Unlike other sports where natural athleticism could mask flaws, golf demanded attention to detail. It required patience, focus, and emotional control qualities that Luke seemed to possess instinctively. He became absorbed by the rhythm of the swing, the feel of the club against the ball, and the subtle strategy behind every shot. At a young age, he began to understand that mastery in golf was not about force but precision, not about bravado but consistency.

As Luke's fascination deepened, his parents recognized that this was more than a passing hobby. They arranged lessons and practice opportunities whenever possible, often sacrificing time and comfort to ensure he could play. Their commitment to nurturing his passion laid the groundwork for what would later become a defining trait of Luke's own character: loyalty and appreciation for those who helped him succeed. His brother, Christian, became his earliest playing partner and, later, a significant influence on his development. The two boys shared countless hours practicing together, sometimes in less-than-ideal conditions, driven by competition and camaraderie.

As Luke entered his teenage years, his technical refinement became more apparent. Coaches noticed his composure and ability to focus for long stretches. He was not the strongest player physically, but his control and short game were exceptional. He displayed the patience of a player twice his age. Each round seemed to reveal more of his unique temperament: calm under pressure, analytical in thought, and deliberate in movement. Local tournaments began to feature his name more frequently, and word spread that the quiet boy from Hertfordshire possessed an unusual gift.

Golf, for Luke, was never a noisy pursuit. He did not seek the spotlight, and he never displayed arrogance. His confidence came from preparation, from countless hours of repetition, and from a belief that excellence required discipline more than raw talent. Friends from his early years recall how he would spend extra time perfecting a single aspect of his game, often after others had packed up and gone home. His passion was not flamboyant; it was focused, steady, and unrelenting. That quiet determination would one day distinguish him from many of his contemporaries, especially in a sport that often rewarded power over precision.

As he approached the end of his secondary education, Luke's future began to take shape more clearly. His performance in junior tournaments caught the attention of scouts and coaches, and opportunities for higher-level play started to appear. Yet, the path ahead was uncertain. Golf was not the most accessible sport for young British players aiming for global success. The infrastructure and resources available to young talents were limited compared to the opportunities available in the United States. For Luke to reach his potential, he would need to move beyond his familiar environment and test himself against stronger competition abroad.

Before that step, though, there was a formative period during which he learned the deeper lessons of sport: humility in victory, grace in defeat, and the unwavering pursuit of consistency. His coaches often remarked that Luke's attitude set him apart. He approached every challenge as a problem to solve rather than a battle to win. This mindset reflected not only his personality but also his upbringing. His parents' quiet strength and his brother's companionship had created a foundation of stability that allowed Luke to thrive in environments where others might have been overwhelmed.

The young golfer's technical skill continued to mature alongside his growing sense of identity. He began to study the techniques of established professionals, watching their form, their approach to pressure, and their decision-making on the course. He admired players who displayed control and finesse rather than sheer aggressive men like Nick Faldo, whose calculated style resonated with Luke's natural tendencies. Faldo's success showed that golf could be mastered through mental precision as much as physical strength. It reinforced Luke's belief that greatness was achievable through discipline and intellect.

The more Luke studied the game, the more he appreciated its psychological depth. Golf, he realized, was not merely a physical test but a mental examination of character. Each shot required total commitment, and every mistake offered an opportunity to learn. The course itself became a teacher, demanding respect and patience. He learned to read the subtleties of terrain, to feel the changes in wind, and to adapt his rhythm accordingly. His developing artistry, the sense that every round was a performance requiring composure and balance, began to take shape during these crucial years.

His entry into more competitive circuits required not only talent but resilience. Traveling to tournaments, competing against stronger and older players, and managing the pressure of expectations tested his resolve. Yet, Luke rarely appeared flustered. He carried himself with the composure of someone who understood that long-term success required more than bursts of brilliance. Those who observed him during his early competitions noticed his maturity. Even when he played poorly, he analyzed his mistakes without visible frustration. His calm demeanor and sportsmanship attracted respect, setting the tone for the professional reputation he would later build.

The decision to pursue golf at an international level was a pivotal one for Luke and his family. Opportunities in the United States, particularly through collegiate golf scholarships, offered a path that could transform a promising young English golfer into a world-class athlete. Luke's academic strength and discipline made him an ideal candidate for such programs. The possibility of studying while refining his game appealed to his balanced mindset. Northwestern University, under the guidance of coach Pat Goss, became the destination that would shape not only his golf career but his entire philosophy toward the sport.

Before leaving for America, Luke had already built a reputation as one of Britain's most promising young golfers. His victories in junior tournaments demonstrated consistency and precision, and his reputation as a methodical, mentally strong competitor spread among coaches and peers. Yet, he remained humble, aware that success in golf was never permanent. Every victory carried lessons, and every setback was a reminder of the game's unforgiving nature. This grounded attitude made him a natural leader even before he reached professional ranks.

Those early years in England provided more than just technical grounding; they built emotional resilience. The small-town courses, the unpredictable weather, and the absence of glamour shaped a player who valued the essence of the sport itself. Luke's connection to golf was deeply personal, a relationship between mind, body, and nature. The fairways of his youth were not merely training grounds but sanctuaries where he could express himself with clarity and purpose. That bond between player and game would never leave him, no matter how high he rose in the rankings or how bright the spotlight became.

Friends and mentors often recall his humility during this stage of life. Despite his growing success, Luke never carried himself as though he were destined for greatness. He approached each day as an opportunity to improve incrementally. This perspective not only kept him grounded but also made him adaptable to the challenges that awaited him abroad. His family's influence was central to this outlook. Colin and Ann instilled a sense of responsibility and gratitude that remained with him throughout his career. Christian's role was equally significant; his later work as a caddie and coach in professional golf deepened their shared understanding of the game's complexities.

Luke's personality during these years reflected a rare balance between quiet intensity and warmth. He could be intensely focused when practicing yet kind and approachable away from the course. This duality would later become a hallmark of his public image, the composed competitor and the gentleman off the course. It also foreshadowed his leadership qualities, which would later emerge fully during his time as a Ryder Cup player and captain.

By the time Luke left England for Northwestern University, he had already established the core identity that would define his entire career: precision over power, thoughtfulness over aggression, composure over chaos. The foundation laid during his youth was not built on sudden breakthroughs but on thousands of deliberate, mindful repetitions. Each moment spent perfecting his swing, each quiet round played under gray English skies, and each word of encouragement from his family became part of the mosaic that formed his professional ethos.

Those early experiences also instilled in Luke an appreciation for beauty and artistry values that would later manifest not only in his playing style but also in his passion for visual art and design. Golf, for him, was an aesthetic pursuit as much as a competitive one. Every shot had to possess rhythm and purpose. This artistic sensibility set him apart from many of his peers and earned him admiration from fans who appreciated his elegant approach to the game.

When reflecting on Luke Donald's rise to global prominence, it is clear that the roots of his success reach back to these formative years. The lessons learned on humble courses, the values instilled by family, and the mindset shaped by patience and precision all converged to create a golfer of extraordinary refinement. The boy from Hemel Hempstead did not dream of overpowering the game; he dreamed of mastering it through understanding and artistry. That dream began to take real form in the English countryside, carried forward by a family who believed that character mattered as much as talent.

By the time Luke stood on the threshold of collegiate competition, he was more than a promising athlete; he was a craftsman of his own destiny. The calmness that would later define his presence under the pressures of professional golf was already deeply ingrained. The emotional steadiness, the commitment to perfection, and the quiet confidence that inspired teammates and rivals alike were born from those early experiences in the heart of England. His journey was only beginning, but the essence of the champion he would become had already taken shape.

Every great athlete's story begins somewhere unassuming a backyard, a local field, a neighborhood club. For Luke Donald, it began with a child's curiosity and a family's belief in patience and integrity. The boy who once studied the rhythm of a perfect swing would one day embody it, earning admiration not through spectacle but through substance. The roots of his greatness were not built on noise or notoriety but on quiet precision, discipline, and love for a game that rewards those who respect its subtleties. Those early days in Hertfordshire would forever remain the unseen foundation of a career that placed a British maestro at the very heart of global golf.

Chapter 2: Swinging into Promise

The transformation from a talented young golfer into a player of genuine potential often occurs quietly, beneath the surface of competition and outside the glare of public attention. For Luke Donald, this stage of development was marked by refinement, growth, and a deepening sense of purpose. The calm, curious child who once studied his swing on modest English fairways evolved into a composed teenager capable of executing under pressure with remarkable control. As he matured, his golf began to take on a distinctive character not loud or flamboyant, but deliberate, elegant, and exacting.

During his adolescent years, Luke's passion for the game deepened into a disciplined commitment. Practice sessions were no longer casual routines; they became laboratories for precision. Every shot was analyzed, every adjustment made with intention. He began to see golf not only as a sport but as an art form that demanded emotional intelligence as much as physical ability. Hours spent on the practice green honed his sense of touch, while countless repetitions from the bunker taught him the subtlety required to control trajectory and spin. The more he practiced, the more his confidence grew, not from bravado but from the quiet assurance that mastery was possible through devotion to detail.

His growing proficiency attracted attention from coaches who recognized something special in his demeanor. Unlike many of his peers who relied on raw athleticism or streaks of brilliance, Luke's progress was measured and systematic. He approached the game with a craftsman's patience, working tirelessly to reduce errors and elevate consistency. Observers noted his calm posture even during intense competition, an indication of mental resilience uncommon for his age. This composure would later become his defining attribute, allowing him to thrive in environments where others faltered under scrutiny.

As his teenage years unfolded, Luke began to compete more regularly in regional and national amateur tournaments. Each event presented a new test, both technically and emotionally. The fields were stronger, the expectations higher, and the margins for error slimmer. Yet he thrived under these conditions. His natural rhythm and commitment to precision made him a difficult opponent, and his ability to recover from setbacks gave him a psychological advantage. Whether battling wind, uneven greens, or the nerves that accompany competitive play, Luke displayed a serenity that drew admiration from coaches and competitors alike.

A key turning point during this period came when he began to refine his swing under structured coaching programs. The focus shifted from basic mechanics to intricate technical optimization: the relationship between tempo, alignment, and timing. Luke embraced this stage of development with the same curiosity that had driven his early passion. He studied his own motion with analytical rigor, identifying micro-adjustments that could yield marginal gains. His teachers quickly recognized his aptitude for understanding instruction not as commands but as concepts to be internalized.

The golf swing, for Luke, became an expression of personality. It mirrored his temperament, balanced, rhythmic, and understated. Coaches often commented that watching him strike the ball was like observing choreography; each movement was purposeful, devoid of wasted energy. His compact form and fluid tempo contrasted sharply with the growing power-driven culture that was beginning to define modern golf. While many young players sought distance at any cost, Luke focused on precision and repeatability. This approach aligned perfectly with his strategic mind and foreshadowed his success in controlling scoring through accuracy rather than brute strength.

The competitive experiences of this era taught him more than technique. They shaped his understanding of pressure, expectation, and resilience. Each round offered lessons about decision-making under stress, about managing energy across long tournaments, and about handling the emotional ebb and flow of competition. Mistakes no longer carried frustration; they became data points in his ongoing pursuit of perfection. Coaches often remarked that his emotional intelligence was far beyond his years. He had the ability to detach from a bad shot without losing his rhythm, a skill that many seasoned professionals still struggled to master.

As his reputation grew, so did his exposure to higher levels of competition. Representing his county and later national amateur teams, he encountered players from across the United Kingdom who shared his ambitions. These experiences widened his perspective and ignited a hunger to measure himself against the best. He began to understand that success required not only technical excellence but also strategic awareness and the ability to adapt one's game to different courses, climates, and psychological environments. Each tournament tested his adaptability, and he developed a reputation for performing well on varied terrains, from narrow parkland layouts to open, windswept links.

One of the defining qualities that emerged during this phase was his methodical approach to preparation. Luke's pre-round routines became almost ritualistic. He treated every warm-up session as an opportunity to tune his body and mind to the demands of the day. His precision extended beyond mechanics to include visualization, mental rehearsal, and emotional centering. These practices built a foundation of consistency that would later sustain him through the unpredictable rhythms of professional golf. Observers often noticed how composed he appeared walking to the first tee shoulders relaxed, eyes focused, expression unreadable. It was the demeanor of someone who trusted his preparation completely.

Outside the competitive arena, Luke's life reflected balance and maturity. While golf dominated his focus, he maintained a disciplined academic record and engaged in extracurricular interests that nourished his creativity. His growing fascination with design and aesthetics hinted at a multidimensional personality. He often described golf as an art of balancing a harmony between power and grace, control and freedom. This artistic sensibility began to influence his approach to practice and performance, giving his game an elegance that resonated with spectators and mentors alike.

The relationship between Luke and his brother Christian also evolved during this time. Christian, himself a skilled player, became an important figure in Luke's development. Their bond combined competition with mentorship, and their practice sessions became laboratories of shared learning. They challenged each other, exchanged observations, and refined their techniques together. This sibling dynamic instilled in Luke a respect for collaboration, even within an individual sport. It reinforced the idea that improvement thrives in environments of mutual trust and shared purpose.

As the late 1990s approached, opportunities began to open for young British golfers to explore collegiate golf in the United States. The American system offered structured competition, world-class facilities, and academic pathways that balanced sport and education. For Luke, this represented both an opportunity and a challenge. The idea of leaving home for a new culture, new courses, and a different style of play was daunting, yet he understood that growth required risk. The decision to pursue collegiate golf was not made impulsively; it followed careful consideration and discussions with family, mentors, and coaches.

Before taking that step, Luke sought to strengthen every aspect of his game. He focused heavily on his short game, recognizing that control around the greens often determined outcomes more than raw distance. Hours were spent chipping from varied lies, experimenting with trajectories, and mastering putts from every conceivable angle. His attention to detail bordered on obsession, but it was this obsession that refined his artistry. His ability to visualize shots before execution gave him an edge that separated him from his peers. He began to understand that the difference between good and great was often invisible: a fraction of alignment, a whisper of tempo, a moment of mental clarity.

His success in junior championships during this period reflected not only technical excellence but also composure under scrutiny. When facing opponents known for aggression, Luke maintained his rhythm, allowing patience to dismantle their urgency. His strategy often frustrated competitors who relied on forcing errors, only to find that he rarely provided any. Coaches began referring to him as a model of efficiency, a player who seemed to conserve energy while maintaining relentless focus. Spectators observed how he approached every hole as though it were a separate puzzle, studying angles, visualizing trajectories, and executing with quiet confidence.

While his rise was steady, it was not without challenges. Adjusting to tougher fields and higher expectations tested his self-belief. There were tournaments where his precision faltered, where weather conditions or fatigue disrupted his rhythm. Yet he refused to dwell on setbacks. Each disappointment became a case study, an opportunity to refine preparation or adjust mindset. Those close to him noticed that his resilience was not born from defiance but from perspective. He understood that golf was a game of imperfect mastery, one where patience outlasted frustration.

Luke's growing maturity caught the attention of American college recruiters who were scouting international talent. His performance record, combined with his demeanor, made him an ideal candidate for scholarship consideration. Northwestern University, renowned for its strong academic standards and competitive golf program, emerged as a perfect match. Under the guidance of coach Pat Goss, Luke would soon find a mentor whose influence would shape the rest of his career. Yet before departing for the United States, he competed in a final stretch of amateur events that showcased his evolution from promising teenager to elite amateur.

During this pre-collegiate phase, he began to demonstrate leadership qualities that set him apart. Younger players sought his advice, not only for technical tips but also for guidance on managing nerves and maintaining composure. His ability to communicate complex concepts with clarity revealed an emerging teacher's instinct. That calm, articulate nature would later define his captaincy and mentorship roles within professional golf. Even as he prepared to leave for America, Luke's humility remained intact. He often expressed gratitude for the coaches and volunteers who had supported his journey, emphasizing that his progress was built on shared effort rather than individual brilliance.

The anticipation of moving abroad stirred a blend of excitement and introspection. Luke was acutely aware that the American collegiate circuit represented a different level of competition. The courses would be longer, the conditions faster, and the players stronger. Yet he saw this not as intimidation but as opportunity. He believed that true growth required discomfort and that the next stage of his evolution as a golfer would demand exposure to new challenges and cultures. His mindset reflected an awareness that mastery is a lifelong pursuit rather than a destination.

As he prepared to embark on this new chapter, Luke carried with him the lessons learned from his formative years in England. The patience forged through countless hours of practice, the discipline honed through meticulous repetition, and the humility nurtured by his family formed the invisible scaffolding of his character. Yet this next stage would require adaptability and the ability to integrate into a new environment while preserving the essence of what made him unique.

Before his departure, local clubs and mentors celebrated his achievements, proud to see one of their own reach a stage few British amateurs achieved at the time. There was admiration for his talent, but also for his demeanor. Luke had never been a product of hype; he had been built through craftsmanship and quiet perseverance. That steadiness gave those who knew him confidence that he would thrive wherever he went.

The period leading up to his collegiate journey marked a turning point not only in his career but in his identity. The boy who once played under gray English skies had become a disciplined young man ready to test himself on a global stage. His game had matured, his character solidified, and his sense of purpose deepened. The promise that began in quiet practice sessions had grown into something tangible, the foundation of a career that would eventually place him among the most admired golfers of his generation.

As he boarded the plane bound for the United States, Luke carried no illusions of instant success. What he carried instead was conviction, the belief that excellence is earned one swing at a time, through patience, humility, and relentless precision. The young golfer from Hertfordshire was ready to meet the wider world, not with arrogance, but with artistry. The promise that began years earlier was now ready to unfold across oceans, as a British talent prepared to make his mark on the global game.

Chapter 3: Across the Atlantic

When Luke Donald stepped off the plane in the United States, he entered an environment unlike anything he had experienced before. The soft greens of Hertfordshire were replaced by vast, manicured fairways stretching under endless American skies. The scale of the country mirrored the scale of opportunity that awaited him, and with that came the challenge of adaptation. The young golfer who had built his game in quiet British settings now stood at the threshold of a world where competition, culture, and ambition existed at full volume. This was not just a change of geography but a shift in rhythm and awakening to a new kind of sporting reality.

His arrival at Northwestern University in Evanston, Illinois, marked a pivotal moment in both his career and his personal growth. Northwestern's golf program combined academic rigor with athletic excellence, a combination that appealed to Luke's dual passions for discipline and learning. The campus, with its mix of intellectual energy and athletic ambition, became the landscape where his next transformation would take place. The person who had left England as a polished amateur would, over the next few years, evolve into a professional-caliber athlete equipped with the mindset and skill set to thrive on the world stage.

The early days were not without discomfort. Luke had to navigate not only the physical distance from his family but also the cultural shift between British reserve and American expressiveness. The collegiate atmosphere thrived on open confidence, team spirit, and vocal motivation elements that contrasted with his typically understated demeanor. Yet rather than resist the difference, he observed and absorbed. He recognized that adapting did not mean abandoning his identity; it meant expanding it. He began to understand that leadership could take many forms, and quiet assurance could be just as powerful as loud enthusiasm.

The person most instrumental in guiding this transition was Northwestern's golf coach, Pat Goss. Their partnership would become one of the most influential relationships of Luke's career. Goss possessed a sharp understanding of technical detail and an intuitive sense of how to develop talent. He quickly recognized that Luke's precision and discipline were rare, but he also saw that they could be refined to even greater effect. What followed was not a mere coach-athlete arrangement but an intellectual collaboration. Goss dissected Luke's mechanics with surgical attention, working with him to optimize every motion of his swing. They spoke the same language : clarity, geometry, and balance.

Under Goss's mentorship, Luke began to redefine his understanding of what mastery required. Practice sessions took on a new intensity and structure.

Data-driven analysis complemented instinctive feel. Every movement had purpose, every drill had a measurable outcome. Luke thrived in this environment because it appealed to his analytical nature. He was not content to repeat actions mechanically; he wanted to understand cause and effect. The American collegiate system, with its emphasis on continuous performance measurement, suited his appetite for precision.

The competitive schedule at Northwestern was rigorous. College golf in the United States demanded travel across states, exposure to different grass types, and constant adjustments to climate and terrain. For Luke, this was an education in adaptability. The courses varied dramatically lush parkland layouts in the Midwest one week, sunbaked fairways in the South the next. Each environment tested his ability to interpret conditions quickly. He learned to trust his instincts, to make strategic decisions without hesitation, and to maintain emotional equilibrium through the unpredictable flow of collegiate tournaments.

Life off the course offered a different kind of learning. Living among peers from diverse backgrounds expanded his worldview. The dormitories, classrooms, and practice ranges became social laboratories where he learned to navigate friendships, cultural nuance, and shared ambition. Many of his teammates admired his focus, often joking about his almost monastic approach to practice. Yet they also respected him for his consistency and humility. While others fluctuated between brilliance and frustration, Luke maintained steady progress not through bursts of inspiration but through disciplined repetition.

Balancing academic workload with athletic commitment required meticulous time management. Northwestern's academic demands were famously rigorous, and Luke approached his studies with the same dedication that he brought to golf. He often described education as a complement to his sport, sharpening the same analytical faculties that guided his decision-making on the course. His appreciation for art and design deepened during these years, revealing an aesthetic sensibility that paralleled his approach to the game. Golf, he often reflected, was architecture in motion structure, proportion, and grace combined through human expression.

The breakthrough in performance came as his collegiate career gained momentum. Under Goss's guidance, Luke began to harness a new level of technical refinement. His swing became more efficient, his putting stroke more confident, his decision-making sharper. Each victory or near miss reinforced his growing self-belief. His teammates recall how he carried himself with quiet authority, leading not through instruction but through example.

On difficult days, when conditions or competition turned fierce, he radiated calm that steadied the entire team. That unspoken influence became part of Northwestern's identity during his tenure, a culture of professionalism shaped around his presence.

Luke's consistency soon translated into national recognition. He began to dominate collegiate leaderboards, and his scoring averages placed him among the top players in the country. Yet success did not alter his demeanor. While other rising stars basked in attention, he remained grounded, focused on incremental improvement. Reporters who interviewed him during this time often commented on his articulate modesty and his unwillingness to indulge in hype. He viewed every achievement as a checkpoint, not a destination. This restraint reflected not only personal temperament but also his upbringing, where humility and diligence were valued above self-promotion.

The American approach to competition taught him something profound about mental resilience. College tournaments often compressed multiple rounds into short spans, demanding both endurance and adaptability. Unlike the relatively stable environment of junior golf in England, collegiate golf introduced variables that tested patience and focus: jet lag, long bus rides, unpredictable weather, and unfamiliar greens. Luke learned to treat these obstacles not as disruptions but as integral aspects of the profession he aspired to enter. Every challenge became part of the larger discipline of mastery.

His relationship with Goss deepened as they continued to refine both technique and mindset. Goss encouraged Luke to see golf as an evolving process rather than a fixed skill. They dissected rounds in post-competition reviews, analyzing missed opportunities and successful strategies with the precision of engineers. Goss's influence extended beyond the mechanics of play; he also helped Luke cultivate emotional balance, reminding him that control of temperament was often the decisive factor between victory and collapse. Over time, their collaboration evolved into a lasting friendship grounded in mutual respect and shared pursuit of excellence.

As his collegiate achievements accumulated, professional scouts began to take notice. Luke's name circulated among golf analysts who predicted a smooth transition to the professional ranks. Yet he remained cautious, aware that talent alone did not guarantee success beyond the structured environment of college golf. The professional circuit demanded a different level of psychological endurance, solitary travel, media attention, and relentless competition against seasoned players. He understood that his technical precision would need to be matched by emotional durability and strategic patience.

During this period, Luke also began to explore the mental side of performance more deeply. He studied focus techniques, breathing exercises, and visualization strategies that would later become essential tools in his career. The American sports culture's emphasis on mental conditioning appealed to him; it aligned with his belief that mastery required harmony between mind and body. By internalizing these methods, he strengthened his ability to remain composed under mounting pressure. His calm presence on the course became not just a natural trait but a cultivated discipline.

One of the defining features of Luke's collegiate years was his unwavering attention to the short game. While many players chased distance gains through weight training and aggressive swings, he devoted hours to perfecting feel shots, delicate chips, controlled pitches, and mid-range putts. He believed that tournaments were often decided within thirty yards of the hole. This philosophy, born from observation and reinforced by data, became a cornerstone of his success. His peers marveled at his creativity around the greens, often watching in silence as he executed shots that seemed effortless but were the result of tireless practice.

Off the course, Luke's reputation grew as a respected ambassador of the program. Professors praised his work ethic, and teammates described him as a steadying presence who balanced intensity with kindness. His ability to remain focused without becoming insular made him a natural role model. The maturity he displayed earned him respect not only within the athletic department but across the broader university community. To many students, he embodied the ideal of a scholar-athlete disciplined, thoughtful, and quietly ambitious.

By his junior year, Luke had achieved what few international players managed: dominance within an American collegiate system that demanded adaptability and sustained excellence. His victories multiplied, and his statistics placed him among the all-time greats in Northwestern history. Yet beneath the success, he maintained a relentless curiosity. He continued to analyze professional tournaments, studying how players handled pressure and course management. He was particularly drawn to the composure of players like Ben Crenshaw and the strategic intelligence of Tom Kite. He sought to understand not only their technique but their emotional rhythm, how they managed momentum, responded to adversity, and sustained belief across decades.

As graduation approached, discussions about turning professional grew more serious. The transition represented both aspiration and risk. Many talented collegiate players struggled to adapt to the demands of life on tour, the isolation, the logistics, and the business side of sport. Luke approached this decision with his characteristic caution, seeking counsel from Goss, family, and trusted mentors. What distinguished him from many peers was not the scale of his ambition but the clarity of his preparation. He would not rush into professional life without a plan that honored the values that had shaped him: patience, craftsmanship, and purpose.

Before leaving Northwestern, Luke left an imprint that would outlast his tenure. His name became synonymous with excellence, and his influence reshaped how future recruits approached both study and sport. The legacy he built there was not measured solely by trophies but by culture and a standard of professionalism that inspired those who followed. His relationship with Goss remained strong long after graduation, evolving into one of golf's most enduring player-coach partnerships.

As he prepared to take his first steps toward the professional arena, Luke reflected on how profoundly the American experience had shaped him. The young man who once arrived as a quiet English amateur had become a mature competitor fluent in the language of elite performance. The journey had not diluted his British composure; it had enhanced it, surrounding it with new layers of tactical intelligence and emotional poise.

Crossing the Atlantic had not simply transported him to a new continent, it had expanded his capacity for growth. The lessons learned on unfamiliar soil, the mentorship that refined his talent, and the resilience built through relentless testing all combined to create a player ready for the world stage. The chapters that awaited him in professional golf would demand every ounce of that preparation.

But beneath the surface of technical mastery and competitive success lay something deeper: a philosophy that had taken root on both sides of the ocean.

That philosophy would define the way Luke Donald approached every challenge that followed — not through spectacle or showmanship, but through grace, calculation, and artistry. The Atlantic that once separated his beginnings from his destiny had become a bridge, linking the calm precision of his English roots with the bold ambition of American competition. From that fusion emerged not just a golfer of remarkable skill, but a craftsman destined to leave a lasting mark on the global stage.

Chapter 4: Turning Pro and Taking Aim

The decision to turn professional marked a defining crossroads in Luke Donald's journey, a point where youthful potential met the formidable realities of global competition. The structured environment of collegiate golf, where routines were supported by coaches, teammates, and predictable schedules, gave way to a solitary path defined by self-reliance and the pursuit of excellence under relentless scrutiny. Every professional athlete must confront the moment when aspiration becomes livelihood, and for Luke, that moment arrived with both excitement and gravity. He was stepping into a world where precision was measured not in academic grades or amateur rankings, but in strokes gained, sponsorship contracts, and leaderboard positions.

Transitioning from amateur to professional status is rarely seamless, even for players of exceptional pedigree. The game itself remains the same, the same greens, the same clubs, the same unforgiving laws of physics yet everything surrounding it changes. Expectations swell, the pressure multiplies, and the margin for error vanishes. Luke approached this transition with characteristic deliberation. He did not rush his debut nor allow external voices to dictate his timeline. After graduating from Northwestern University, he spent reflective months preparing his body, refining his routines, and strengthening his mental framework for the challenges ahead. He knew that once he teed off as a professional, there would be no safety net, no structured collegiate circuit to fall back on. Every swing would count toward building or breaking his reputation.

The path to professional golf runs through qualifying schools, developmental tours, and invitation-only events where the finest amateurs test their skills against seasoned veterans. These tournaments can be unforgiving, exposing weaknesses that even consistent collegiate players struggle to conceal. Luke entered this environment with awareness and respect. His preparation with coach Pat Goss had honed not only his mechanics but also his self-awareness. He knew precisely where his strengths lay: a world-class short game, impeccable control, and the temperament to thrive under pressure. Yet he also understood that professional golf demanded a broader arsenal. Distance, endurance, and adaptability would be critical if he was to succeed across diverse courses and climates.

When he officially declared professional status, expectations from both sides of the Atlantic began to form. British media saw in him a potential successor to the technical artistry of players like Nick Faldo. American observers, familiar with his collegiate dominance, viewed him as a model of discipline and intelligence. Luke was conscious of these perceptions but refused to let them define his focus. He believed that public acclaim could distract from the deeper work of mastery. His goal was not to impress headlines but to earn credibility through consistency.

The first months on tour brought both promise and humility. Professional circuits are a crucible where even prodigious talent faces reality checks. Luke experienced the challenges that confront every newcomer: the grind of travel, the loneliness of hotel rooms, the adjustments to time zones, and the financial uncertainty that shadows young players before sponsorships materialize. He learned to manage logistics with precision, keeping schedules tight and training consistent. His analytical mindset proved valuable; he treated every event as a case study, tracking performance metrics, identifying trends, and refining his strategy after each round.

His early tournaments revealed flashes of brilliance. The same composure that had defined his collegiate career now served him well against established competitors. Crowds began to notice his elegant rhythm and his measured approach to every shot. Commentators described him as "the quiet craftsman," a player who seemed immune to emotional turbulence. Yet beneath the calm exterior lay relentless ambition. He was not content to make cuts; he aimed to contend. Each competitive outing became an opportunity to learn from seasoned professionals, to study how they managed fatigue, controlled pace, and maintained sharpness through long seasons.

Earning status on the major tours required perseverance. The process demanded strong finishes across qualifying events and selective invitations.

Luke's combination of discipline and precision gradually earned him recognition among tour organizers. His breakthrough came when he began securing top-ten finishes that placed him on the radar of sponsors and ranking systems. Those performances were not the result of sudden transformation but of meticulous groundwork laid years earlier. His training routines under Goss emphasized repeatability, ensuring that even under pressure, his swing remained consistent. That reliability became his greatest weapon; he could trust his motion under the harshest conditions.

Success in professional golf often hinges on the ability to handle volatility. A single poor round can erase the work of an entire tournament. Luke's calm nature allowed him to navigate such swings without panic. He viewed each hole as a fresh challenge, unaffected by previous mistakes or fleeting triumphs. Observers began to note his mental fortitude, his capacity to stay present regardless of circumstance. That psychological steadiness distinguished him from peers who fluctuated between brilliance and frustration. His maturity became evident not only in his results but also in the respect he commanded from fellow players.

Behind the scenes, the realities of professional life began to reveal themselves. Luke now bore responsibility for building a support network of caddies, fitness specialists, physiotherapists, and management professionals to handle contracts and sponsorships. Selecting the right people required intuition and trust. The relationships forged during this stage would influence his career trajectory as profoundly as his technical choices. He prioritized collaboration with individuals who shared his values: discipline, loyalty, and quiet excellence. This emphasis on character mirrored his own personality and contributed to the cohesion that defined his team throughout his career.

As his performances improved, his profile grew. Media interviews became part of his new routine, offering glimpses into a personality that remained understated yet articulate. He spoke about golf with the same clarity he brought to playing it precise, thoughtful, and devoid of theatrics. Fans found in him a refreshing contrast to the more flamboyant figures of the sport. His professionalism resonated particularly with young players who admired his dedication to the craft rather than to celebrity. Yet behind the controlled image lay the constant battle all professionals face: maintaining confidence through fluctuating form and the unpredictable dynamics of competition.

One of Luke's earliest lessons on tour involved the emotional weight of expectations. Success breeds attention, and attention breeds pressure. With each promising finish, the anticipation of victory intensified. He learned that the ability to manage external noise was as vital as controlling tempo on a swing. Some tournaments tested his patience, with near-misses reminding him how fine the margins were at the top level. Yet these moments also reinforced his resilience. He refused to interpret setbacks as failure; they became fuel for refinement. His long-term mindset allowed him to stay focused on progression rather than short-term results.

Technically, Luke's game continued to evolve. His work with Goss incorporated cutting-edge analysis, including video breakdowns and biomechanical assessments that were innovative for the time. The goal was not to overhaul his swing but to sharpen its efficiency. The emphasis remained on alignment, rhythm, and tempo, the cornerstones of his identity as a precision player. This analytical approach complemented his artistic instincts, blending science and feel into a seamless methodology. Observers often remarked that his swing appeared effortless, but that grace was the product of thousands of hours of disciplined repetition.

The professional environment also deepened his understanding of strategy. He began to approach tournaments with an architect's mindset, studying course designs, wind patterns, and pin placements with meticulous care. His attention to preparation became legendary among peers. Caddies appreciated his ability to discuss angles and trajectories with mathematical clarity. Unlike players who relied purely on instinct, Luke combined intuition with calculation. Every hole was dissected into probabilities, and every decision stemmed from analysis rather than impulse. This methodical style mirrored his personality and earned him a reputation as one of the game's most cerebral competitors.

As his confidence solidified, so too did his ambition. He began setting clear performance goals, focusing not merely on participation but on progression through rankings. Each event was approached as part of a long-term structure rather than an isolated challenge. He analyzed statistics relentlessly greens in regulation, putts per round, proximity to the hole searching for incremental gains. His drive for improvement was quiet but unyielding. He did not chase transformation through radical change but through consistent refinement.

The financial aspects of professional golf also introduced new complexities. Tournament earnings, sponsorships, and endorsements became integral to sustaining his career. Luke approached these responsibilities with prudence, treating contracts as extensions of professionalism rather than vanity. He aligned with brands that reflected his values: quality, discipline, and understated sophistication. This strategic alignment reinforced his image as a modern gentleman of the sport, blending traditional sportsmanship with contemporary sensibility.

During his early seasons, travel became both exhilarating and exhausting. Weeks spent crossing continents, adjusting to climates, and maintaining focus amidst jet lag tested his endurance. Yet Luke approached travel with structure. He scheduled rest deliberately, balanced training intensity, and maintained dietary discipline to preserve energy. His attention to recovery reflected his broader philosophy that success required equilibrium the synchronization of physical, mental, and emotional systems.

As victories began to accumulate, so did recognition from within the golfing community. Commentators praised his short game, describing it as one of the most technically refined in the sport. His ability to control spin, judge pace, and read greens with uncanny accuracy made him a formidable competitor on any surface. Fellow professionals spoke of his sportsmanship and consistency. He rarely showed frustration, even under immense pressure. That composure became part of his legend, symbolizing the idea that mastery need not be loud to be powerful.

Moments of triumph often arrived quietly for Luke, without grand gestures or dramatic celebrations. He would raise his cap politely, acknowledge the crowd, and return to reflection. His victories felt like affirmations of process rather than explosions of emotion. Fans began to associate him with elegance, the kind of grace that transcended results and spoke to the spirit of the game itself.

As seasons unfolded, Luke established himself as a steady presence across both the PGA and European Tours. His transatlantic background made him uniquely adaptable, able to navigate the differing styles of play on either side of the ocean. American courses rewarded strategic precision and consistency, while European layouts demanded creativity in adverse weather. Luke thrived in both, his balanced temperament serving as an equalizer against environmental challenges. His rise through world rankings was not meteoric but methodical, a reflection of his philosophy that excellence is built through patience and discipline rather than spectacle.

The grind of tour life forged deeper resilience. There were stretches where his form dipped, where putts lipped out and confidence wavered. Yet those periods revealed his inner fortitude. He analyzed patterns, sought feedback, and refused to surrender to frustration. His relationship with Goss remained a stabilizing anchor. The two communicated constantly, refining mechanics and mindset, ensuring that every setback became an opportunity for recalibration. That continuity of mentorship provided emotional steadiness in a world where careers often swung between extremes.

Luke's emergence as a respected figure among peers extended beyond performance. Younger players gravitated toward him for guidance, drawn by his intellect and authenticity. He shared insights freely, emphasizing patience and respect for the game's traditions. His demeanor reflected an understanding that success was fleeting unless grounded in values. This quiet leadership would later evolve into his influence as a Ryder Cup player and captain, but its origins were visible during these formative professional years.

By the time his reputation as a global competitor was fully established, Luke had achieved what few British players of his generation managed seamless integration into both the American and European circuits. His career trajectory represented the synthesis of two cultures, two schools of golf thought, and two expressions of mastery. He embodied the balance between scientific precision and creative artistry, between technical rigor and emotional grace.

Turning professional had not been a leap into the unknown but a carefully measured step toward self-realization. The lessons learned during these early years extended far beyond mechanics or rankings. They forged the psychological architecture of a champion one who viewed competition as a dialogue with himself rather than a battle against others. The quiet discipline that had defined his childhood and the analytical depth cultivated in America now converged into a mature identity.

As Luke Donald moved through his early professional seasons, the outlines of greatness became visible. His poise under pressure, his elegance of movement, and his devotion to excellence began to shape a narrative that transcended sport. He was no longer the promising English amateur or the collegiate standout; he had become a craftsman on the grandest stage, a golfer whose pursuit of perfection resonated not through noise but through the subtle harmony of skill and soul. The boy from Hertfordshire had arrived, not as a comet blazing briefly across the sky, but as a steady light destined to guide a generation toward a more thoughtful, artful expression of the game.

Chapter 5: Climbing the World Rankings

Reaching the summit of world golf is not a sudden event; it is a gradual ascent shaped by thousands of precise movements, measured risks, and the persistent refusal to yield. For Luke Donald, the journey toward becoming the world's top-ranked golfer was defined by meticulous progression. Every round, every tournament, and every adjustment built upon a foundation of calculated intent. His rise was not characterized by dramatic bursts of dominance but by unwavering excellence across seasons. That consistency became his identity, the quiet rhythm of progress that distinguished him from contemporaries who soared and fell with unpredictable volatility.

As Luke entered the prime years of his professional career, his understanding of competition evolved. The early struggles of adapting to tour life had tempered him. He no longer played merely to belong; he played to shape outcomes, to set standards that reflected his vision of mastery. The shift was subtle but transformative. He began each tournament with a sense of ownership and awareness that he was not an outsider seeking validation but a contender capable of controlling his destiny. The mental refinement of this period became the engine behind his climb through the global rankings.

Tournament schedules for elite golfers are grueling, a relentless rotation across continents that demands physical stamina and mental clarity. Luke approached this demanding cycle with precision. Each event was planned with strategic purpose. He chose courses that suited his style layouts that rewarded accuracy, intelligent course management, and touch around the greens. This targeted approach allowed him to maximize performance without overextending his energy. He treated rest as an element of preparation, balancing competition with recovery to maintain peak form. His discipline in scheduling contrasted with players who chased every opportunity, often at the expense of long-term stability.

The early signs of his ascent were visible through statistical patterns. His scoring averages began to align with those of established champions. On leaderboards, his name appeared with increasing regularity near the top. He developed a reputation for converting pressure into composure. When others faltered under Sunday tension, he remained calm, methodical, and deliberate. Observers began to describe his performance as clinical, not cold, but controlled, a demonstration of how intellect and technique could coexist within an emotionally charged sport. That emotional balance became one of his defining characteristics, earning him admiration from peers who recognized the difficulty of maintaining clarity under constant scrutiny.

Consistency became Luke's greatest weapon. While power hitters often captured attention with explosive drives, his precision told a quieter story. He excelled at shaping shots to fit the course rather than forcing the course to bend to his will. His short game, already among the finest in the world, became a tool for recovery and attack alike. On courses where others struggled with unpredictable lies or tricky greens, Luke thrived. His control of trajectory and spin allowed him to craft solutions others couldn't envision. That creativity, born from countless hours of practice, gave him an edge that translated into cumulative success.

Each tournament became a chapter in his progression. There were victories that validated his methods, and there were near-misses that fueled his refinement. He did not allow frustration to linger;

every result was data, every challenge an opportunity to evolve. His analytical approach turned setbacks into lessons. He dissected rounds with scientific rigor, identifying where fractions of strokes could be saved through smarter choices. Over time, those marginal gains accumulated into substantial advantage. The global ranking system, which rewards consistent excellence, became a mirror of his philosophy. He didn't need streaks of dominance; he needed sustained brilliance, and that was precisely what he delivered.

The psychological component of climbing the rankings cannot be overstated. Golf is an individual sport, yet success often depends on navigating invisible pressures expectations from sponsors, media, and self-imposed standards. Luke handled these pressures with an almost philosophical calm. He maintained perspective, viewing each event as a test of process rather than proof of worth. This detachment shielded him from the emotional turbulence that derails even talented players. His mindset reflected the poise of a man who valued integrity of effort above fleeting recognition. That emotional equilibrium became central to his ability to perform consistently across varying conditions.

As his profile grew, media narratives began to evolve. Commentators no longer spoke of him as the promising Englishman or the reliable competitor. They began to call him elite part of a small cadre capable of contending on any stage. His demeanor, measured and thoughtful, made him an intriguing figure in a sport that often celebrates flamboyance. He became a symbol of sophistication, embodying the idea that greatness could be achieved through subtle mastery rather than aggression. Fans appreciated the purity of his technique, while fellow professionals respected the quiet authority he carried within each round.

The balance between technical refinement and mental strength defined this period of Luke's career. On the range, he worked tirelessly on repetition, focusing on micro-adjustments that enhanced stability under pressure. His practice sessions were structured around simulation replicating the intensity of competition through deliberate scenarios. This approach built resilience into his performance. He trained not just to hit perfect shots but to recover from imperfection. That distinction separated him from those who chased aesthetic perfection without preparing for adversity.

The physical conditioning that supported his rise was another aspect of his evolution. Recognizing that modern golf demanded athletic endurance, Luke committed to fitness regimens that enhanced flexibility, balance, and durability. His workouts emphasized stability and control over sheer strength. The goal was not to transform his physique but to fortify the foundation of his swing. That physical preparation minimized injuries and allowed him to maintain performance over prolonged seasons. The result was a player who could compete across diverse conditions without fatigue eroding precision.

Traveling between continents required adaptability not just in logistics but in mindset. Time zones, climates, and cultural contrasts introduced constant variables. Luke developed rituals to maintain continuity meditation, journaling, and structured routines that anchored him regardless of environment. These habits preserved focus when schedules blurred and distractions multiplied. His discipline in maintaining equilibrium amid the chaos of global touring reflected his understanding that mastery was as much about self-management as technical skill.

As victories accumulated, so did respect within the locker rooms. Peers recognized him not only for his shot-making but for his professionalism. He carried himself with humility, treating every opponent with quiet respect. Younger players observed his conduct and often sought his advice on handling tour pressures. His responses were thoughtful, rooted in experience rather than theory. He emphasized patience, preparation, and integrity qualities that transcended sport. That mentorship role would later become more formal, but its seeds were planted during this period of personal and professional maturity.

The climb toward the world number one ranking was gradual yet relentless. Each season brought him closer. His finishes in major tournaments solidified credibility; his performances in regular events demonstrated dependability. The statistical models that calculated rankings began reflecting his dominance in consistency metrics, cuts made, scoring averages, top-ten finishes. Analysts noted that his steadiness across surfaces and continents was unmatched. While others oscillated between peaks and valleys, Luke's trajectory was a smooth ascent built on precision, composure, and strategy.

There came a point when his proximity to the top became inevitable. The global golf community watched with anticipation as he closed the gap separating him from the pinnacle. When he finally ascended to the number one position, it was not accompanied by flamboyant celebration. His reaction reflected the same humility that had guided him throughout his journey. He viewed the achievement not as arrival but as affirmation of years of dedication. The emotion lay beneath the surface pride tempered by gratitude and a deep awareness of the responsibility that came with the title.

Holding that position introduced new dimensions of challenge. Remaining at the summit is often harder than reaching it. The scrutiny intensified; every performance was measured against the expectations of a world leader. Luke approached this phase with characteristic balance. He refused to alter his preparation or chase validation through spectacle. Instead, he doubled down on the process focusing on the controllable elements that had brought him success. His defense of the top ranking became a masterclass in composure under pressure, proof that discipline could withstand the turbulence of global attention.

The years at the peak represented the culmination of his philosophy. His achievements were not products of extraordinary physicality but of precision, patience, and intellect. He became a symbol of how methodical excellence could prevail in an era dominated by power. Younger players studied his approach, analyzing how he converted consistency into supremacy. His presence at the top reshaped perceptions of what defined a champion. For fans and analysts alike, he embodied a version of greatness rooted in grace rather than aggression.

His influence extended beyond leaderboards. Sponsors and organizations admired his professionalism, making him a sought-after ambassador for the sport. He used this visibility responsibly, promoting values of respect, integrity, and continuous improvement. His interviews often reflected introspection rather than self-promotion. He spoke about the artistry of golf, the balance between control and creativity, and the emotional intelligence required to perform under scrutiny. This thoughtful communication deepened his connection with audiences who saw in him not just a competitor but a craftsman of life's discipline.

During this era, his performances in team events like the Ryder Cup amplified his reputation as a dependable force. Representing Europe, he delivered under immense pressure, contributing crucial points and displaying leadership that inspired teammates. His ability to remain composed while carrying national expectations mirrored his individual mindset. Those experiences reinforced his belief that golf's essence lay in collaboration as much as individuality. The camaraderie of team competition provided emotional balance to the solitary demands of professional touring.

Maintaining motivation after reaching the top is often a psychological test. Luke's motivation stemmed from the pursuit of refinement rather than the preservation of status. He continued to seek small enhancements, improvements in putting alignment, adjustments in pre-shot routine, optimizations in mental preparation. His hunger for incremental progress kept complacency at bay. Each day became an opportunity to extend mastery rather than defend achievement. That mindset distinguished him from champions who plateau after reaching their goals.

Critics sometimes questioned his lack of overwhelming distance off the tee, yet that critique missed the essence of his strategy. He proved that golf was not purely a contest of power but of intelligence and precision. His success validated the principle that control could outthink force. By adhering to his authentic style, he challenged the sport's evolving narrative and reminded fans of golf's nuanced artistry. This integrity to self became part of his legacy, an enduring message to aspiring players that authenticity is a competitive strength.

As time progressed, the strain of maintaining elite performance became apparent. The sport's younger generation brought fresh intensity, new technologies, and different philosophies. Yet Luke remained competitive through adaptability. He did not resist evolution but absorbed innovation selectively, filtering trends through his principles. His openness to growth without sacrificing identity reflected his intellectual depth. That flexibility allowed him to remain relevant even as the landscape shifted toward athletic explosiveness.

Reflection became a natural byproduct of sustained success. Luke often spoke of gratitude for family, mentors, and the opportunity to pursue excellence at the highest level. Those reflections did not signal complacency but perspective. He understood the rarity of his accomplishments and the collective effort behind them. The humility that had marked his early years persisted, grounding him through accolades and challenges alike.

As his reign at the top transitioned into a phase of enduring influence, the essence of his climb remained clear: it was never about dominance but about devotion. He had reached the highest ranking through a philosophy that valued steadiness over spectacle, intelligence over intimidation, and mastery over momentary triumph. His journey redefined success as a product of harmony between mind, body, and spirit.

The climb through the world rankings was more than a professional trajectory; it was an artistic composition played in measured tempo. Each shot, each decision, each moment of restraint contributed to a symphony of precision that resonated beyond sport. Luke Donald's ascent became a testament to what can be achieved when ambition aligns with discipline, when purpose transcends ego, and when excellence is pursued not for applause but for the quiet satisfaction of knowing one has given the game everything it deserves. Through his rise, golf witnessed the enduring truth that greatness does not always shout, sometimes it whispers, with perfect control, across the greens of the world.

Chapter 6: Rivalries, Respect, and the Ryder Cup

The Ryder Cup stands as one of sport's most electric theaters, a collision between individual brilliance and collective identity, where national pride merges with personal ambition, and where legends are not measured by prize money but by the roar of teammates and fans united under a single flag. For Luke Donald, this arena became both a proving ground and a sanctuary. It offered him the rare opportunity to merge his meticulous discipline with the raw passion of team competition. The quiet craftsman, so often reserved and inwardly focused, transformed under the banner of Europe into a figure of steadfast composure and unshakeable belief. The event brought out layers of his character that individual tournaments could never fully reveal.

When Luke first earned his place on the European Ryder Cup team, it marked not just personal achievement but a validation of years of consistency. Representing Europe against the might of the United States carried a different kind of gravity. It was not about rankings or endorsements; it was about trust being chosen to carry the hopes of a continent in an emotionally charged rivalry that spanned decades. For a golfer whose game was defined by precision and patience, the unpredictable intensity of match play introduced a fresh dimension. Here, he was not playing against the course; he was facing another competitor directly, hole by hole, with every shot echoing through crowds draped in blue and red.

From his debut, Luke displayed a temperament perfectly suited for the format. The head-to-head nature of the matches demanded poise under pressure, quick adaptation, and emotional control all of which had become his hallmarks. He thrived in the environment where calculation met courage. His ability to silence the noise around him while maintaining focus on the present shot turned him into one of Europe's most reliable assets. Every putt holed, every approach landing softly near the pin, carried the precision of a surgeon and the calm of a veteran who understood that momentum in match play is built not on aggression but on unwavering consistency.

The European locker room, often a mix of languages, personalities, and playing styles, became a second family for Luke. He found camaraderie among peers who respected his professionalism and his unspoken leadership. Though not the loudest voice, he commanded attention through action. His preparation set a tone; his steadiness provided reassurance during tense moments. Teammates observed how he analyzed courses with quiet diligence, how he mapped strategy sessions with subtle insights that turned into tactical advantages. The Ryder Cup demanded emotional connection, and Luke's quiet reliability made him a pillar within that collective heartbeat.

Rivalries within the competition often drew intense media focus, framing narratives that amplified anticipation. For Luke, these rivalries were not about personal antagonism but about respect for the caliber of opposition. Facing world-class American players who embodied different styles, some built on explosive power, others on fearless putting, forced him to elevate his adaptability. He relished the challenge of dissecting their strengths and finding ways to neutralize them through his own brand of efficiency. Match play magnified his strengths: accuracy off the tee, touch around the greens, and the psychological control that often wore opponents down over time. He did not overpower; he outthought.

The tension of those transatlantic battles transcended sport. Every swing carried historical weight, each pairing symbolized a continuation of decades of rivalry. Luke approached these duels with a blend of intensity and grace, embodying the spirit of competition rooted in respect. American fans, even while cheering against him, often admired his sportsmanship and composure. There was something timeless about his manner, an echo of golf's classical era where decorum stood alongside desire. That dignity, combined with his performance, earned him universal admiration across both teams.

Moments from those Ryder Cups remain etched into the collective memory of the sport. There were matches where he faced ferocious crowds on American soil, where chants and noise sought to rattle European resolve. Luke responded not with bravado but with silence, letting the precision of his game do the talking. Each birdie became an act of quiet defiance, each par save a message that resilience would not be shaken. His teammates drew strength from that demeanor. His calm presence on the course acted as a stabilizing current in the chaos of competition, a reminder that victory often belongs to those who think clearly when emotions run wild.

Partnerships became central to his Ryder Cup legacy. The format often required pairing players of contrasting temperaments and styles. Luke's adaptability made him the ideal partner. Whether playing alongside fiery personalities or introspective tacticians, he adjusted seamlessly. He had an intuitive understanding of rhythm, allowing partnerships to flourish through trust rather than ego. Communication with partners was understated yet precise, a nod here, a brief word there, enough to maintain alignment. His ability to elevate others made him invaluable to captains seeking reliability under duress.

Those who shared fairways with him spoke of his calming influence. His steady pulse under pressure inspired confidence, creating a psychological edge that often tilted matches in Europe's favor. He approached each pairing with humility, prioritizing synergy over personal glory. The scoreboard mattered more than individual accolades. That ethos resonated deeply with the European team culture, where unity was treated as both a strategy and a moral compass. Luke embodied that philosophy perfectly, a reminder that greatness in sport often stems from service to something larger than oneself.

Beyond the matches, the camaraderie of the Ryder Cup environment enriched his career in profound ways. The solitude of individual competition gives way during those weeks to laughter in team rooms, late-night strategy sessions, and the emotional highs and lows shared among peers. Luke cherished those bonds. For a man often described as reserved, the Ryder Cup unlocked a warmth that came from belonging. He connected deeply with captains and teammates, absorbing lessons on leadership, trust, and resilience. Those interactions would later shape his perspective on mentorship and team dynamics, preparing him for his eventual role as captain.

The emotional gravity of victory and defeat within the Ryder Cup cannot be overstated. Luke experienced both the euphoria of triumph when Europe reclaimed the cup and the ache of near misses where victory slipped away. Yet his responses never wavered from grace. In celebration, he remained measured, acknowledging effort before emotion. In defeat, he displayed perspective, recognizing that respect between competitors outlived any scoreboard. This balanced approach earned him admiration not only from fans but from opponents who valued his authenticity.

The rivalries born from those contests were rooted in mutual admiration. Across the Atlantic, several American golfers held Luke in high regard. They understood that behind his calm façade was a fierce competitor who demanded excellence of himself. Conversations off the course revealed intellectual curiosity and humility traits that transcended rivalry. He built friendships that defied the divisiveness of competition, proving that true sportsmanship could coexist with relentless pursuit of victory.

Each Ryder Cup deepened his understanding of pressure and teamwork. The event distilled golf to its emotional essence: unity, courage, and the courage to face the unknown. Standing on the first tee amid deafening chants, Luke learned to channel adrenaline into clarity. He often described those moments as electric yet meditative, a paradox where the outer chaos sharpened inner stillness. That equilibrium became part of his identity, influencing his approach even in individual tournaments afterward.

Leadership within the team naturally evolved around him. Younger players gravitated toward his calmness, seeking guidance on managing nerves and maintaining concentration. He mentored without pretense, sharing strategies grounded in experience. He emphasized visualization, preparation, and the discipline to trust one's process. Those insights became foundational for teammates who later cited his mentorship as instrumental in shaping their mental approach to pressure.

As his career matured, so too did his understanding of legacy. The Ryder Cup was more than competition; it was continuity, a bridge between generations. He saw himself as both custodian and contributor to a tradition that symbolized unity in diversity. The European team's strength had always been its ability to blend cultures into collective purpose, and Luke took pride in being part of that narrative. His reflections on the event often touched upon the human connections that endured beyond the trophies, the friendships, the respect, the shared pursuit of excellence.

His performances in the Cup also elevated his reputation globally. Analysts often pointed to his match-play record as evidence of an extraordinary capacity to handle pressure. Commentators highlighted his consistency, his strategic mind, and his ability to thrive when stakes were highest. He became synonymous with reliability the player captains could count on when the balance of victory teetered. That trust became his hallmark, an embodiment of quiet heroism that contrasted with the flamboyance sometimes associated with the sport.

The respect he earned during those campaigns extended beyond his team. American fans, initially adversarial in spirit, grew to appreciate his professionalism. His refusal to engage in gamesmanship or theatrics stood out in an era where spectacle often dominated headlines. He represented the ideal of competition rooted in honor. The applause he received from opposing galleries, even during losses, testified to his impact. He had transcended rivalry to become a symbol of golf's enduring integrity.

Over time, his contributions evolved from performance to guidance. Captains relied on his insight for pairing strategies and mental preparation. He possessed an uncanny ability to read team dynamics, sensing when a player needed encouragement or space. His empathy, combined with analytical sharpness, made him a natural leader. When the moment arrived for him to serve as captain himself, it felt less like an appointment and more like destiny fulfilled.

As captain, Luke brought the same precision and composure that had defined his playing career. He viewed leadership not as authority but as stewardship. Preparation became his foundation for detailed analysis of opponents, course conditions, and psychological readiness. He infused the team with calm confidence, emphasizing clarity of purpose and collective belief. His communication was measured yet inspiring, focusing on trust and respect rather than fiery speeches. Under his guidance, players felt both supported and empowered.

The intensity of Ryder Cup leadership carries immense emotional weight. Balancing strategy with empathy, managing egos while nurturing unity, requires both tactical and emotional intelligence. Luke's strength lay in his ability to maintain equilibrium amidst the storm. He radiated assurance without arrogance, conviction without rigidity. His players responded to that energy, finding in him a leader who embodied everything the competition represented: courage, humility, and composure under fire.

The enduring significance of his Ryder Cup legacy rests not solely on wins or losses but on the character he brought to every match. He demonstrated that excellence could coexist with kindness, that fierce rivalry need not abandon respect, and that leadership flourishes through quiet conviction rather than volume. His journey through those contests revealed the essence of who he was, a craftsman of both skill and spirit, capable of uniting individuals under shared purpose.

Reflecting on his experiences, Luke often described the Ryder Cup as the purest form of golf's emotional truth. It stripped away the individualism of your life and replaced it with collective identity. Each point earned was a piece of shared history, each handshake across the green a symbol of mutual admiration. Those moments shaped him beyond sport, reminding him that greatness is measured not only in achievements but in the respect one commands through integrity.

The rivalries, friendships, and unforgettable duels forged across those cups became part of Luke Donald's enduring story, a story of balance between solitude and solidarity, of intellect fused with emotion, of mastery anchored in humility. The Ryder Cup revealed that beneath his quiet exterior burned an unrelenting competitive fire, one guided by grace rather than noise. Through those matches, he transformed from a student of the game into one of its finest examples, a man who proved that true greatness resides not in domination but in the respect earned from both allies and adversaries alike.

That legacy continues to echo across fairways and locker rooms, reminding every player that golf, at its heart, remains a dialogue between rivals bound by shared reverence for the game. Luke Donald's name endures within that dialogue not as a man who sought the spotlight, but as one who illuminated it through composure, courage, and the quiet majesty of enduring respect.

Chapter 7: The Art of the Game

Golf, for Luke Donald, was never merely a contest of numbers or distance. It was an expression of precision, rhythm, and creative intuition, a living canvas where each shot reflected a dialogue between calculation and artistry. His approach to the sport elevated it beyond physical mechanics into something closer to music or painting. Every swing carried intention, every decision stemmed from a patient study of nuance. For him, mastery was not defined by power, but by harmony between mind, body, and the unpredictable landscape of a golf course. This philosophy shaped not only his playing style but his entire identity as a professional athlete, giving him a distinction that transcended statistics.

From the earliest days of his career, Luke understood that golf rewarded subtlety as much as strength. While many contemporaries pursued distance and spectacle, he pursued precision. His swing, smooth and controlled, became a visual embodiment of balance. Coaches often remarked that his tempo appeared as though guided by an internal metronome never rushed, never hesitant. This consistency stemmed from his belief that rhythm was the invisible foundation of excellence. He viewed each round as a composition, where flow and timing mattered as much as power. That sense of grace became his signature, setting him apart in an era increasingly defined by velocity and brute force.

His understanding of the short game revealed a depth of imagination that bordered on artistry. The delicacy required around the greens appealed to his instinct for touch and spatial awareness. Where others might rely on mechanical repetition, he visualized trajectories, calculating spin, slope, and grass texture as if solving a living puzzle. Each chip or bunker shot carried an element of storytelling, a small performance in which execution depended on creativity as much as control. Fellow professionals often spoke of his mastery in this realm with reverence, acknowledging that few could match his finesse when pressure tightened and every blade of grass seemed to whisper challenge.

What made his artistry exceptional was his devotion to preparation. He treated practice as an act of craftsmanship rather than routine. Hours on the range were not about volume but about refinement. He analyzed every motion, testing how slight adjustments in grip or stance altered flight patterns. His focus bordered on meditative, an immersion that mirrored the discipline of a sculptor shaping raw material into form. Observers sometimes mistook his calm for detachment, but beneath that quiet exterior burned relentless curiosity, a need to perfect even the smallest detail until it became instinctive.

Luke's relationship with the golf course was deeply personal. He saw landscapes not as obstacles but as partners in creation. Each fairway carried personality, each green a hidden rhythm. His approach blended respect and challenge; he sought not to overpower a course, but to interpret its design with intelligence and grace. That mindset produced an almost poetic connection between player and environment. His shot selections often revealed an artist's eye for geometry and proportion, using angles and trajectories to turn risk into opportunity. Such decisions elevated his play from mechanical execution to expressive dialogue.

His ability to manage pace and tempo reflected an understanding that golf mirrored life's complexities. Patience, restraint, and emotional balance were as essential as skill. When faced with adversity, he seldom displayed frustration. Instead, he treated every setback as information, a clue to refine his response. This temperament, cultivated through years of deliberate practice, allowed him to maintain equilibrium under the most intense scrutiny. Where others might lose composure, he found rhythm within chaos, transforming tension into clarity. That mental strength became an integral part of his artistry, as essential as his swing plane or putting stroke.

The art of the game, as he saw it, was inseparable from self-awareness. Luke believed that performance reflected character the ability to remain honest with one's strengths and limitations. His introspective nature fostered a constant process of adjustment. He never chased trends blindly; instead, he filtered advice through his own philosophy. This discernment protected the authenticity of his technique. It also revealed a deeper truth: mastery is not achieved through imitation but through self-knowledge. Every evolution in his game stemmed from an internal conversation about balance, purpose, and identity.

Technology's rise within golf posed new challenges and opportunities for players like Luke. Data analytics, advanced equipment, and biomechanical insights promised precision, yet he approached these innovations with thoughtful restraint. He respected science but trusted instinct. Numbers could inform, but feel remained irreplaceable. His swing analysis sessions often involved both digital feedback and sensory awareness listening to the sound of impact, studying the shape of flight, noting the tension in his hands. This fusion of modern insight and traditional intuition became a hallmark of his approach, blending intellect with artistry in equal measure.

The psychological dimension of his craft was equally refined. Mental clarity distinguished the greats from the merely talented. Luke cultivated focus through mindfulness techniques long before they became mainstream in sport. Visualization formed a central part of his preparation; he would walk through each hole mentally, rehearsing outcomes before a tournament even began. This exercise allowed him to approach competition with a sense of familiarity, as though each moment had already been lived. The confidence derived from such preparation was not loud but unshakeable, rooted in quiet certainty rather than bravado.

His putting routine epitomized precision through patience. Many observers marveled at his ability to read greens with uncanny accuracy. He studied contours with a painter's eye, tracing invisible lines between ball and cup. His pre-shot rituals were consistent, a sequence of breaths and gestures designed to anchor concentration. The motion itself smooth, deliberate, rhythmic seemed to defy pressure. To watch him putt during critical moments was to witness mastery distilled into stillness. The hole often seemed to widen when he stepped up, not because of luck but because of the purity of his focus.

A defining aspect of his artistry lay in restraint. Modern golf often celebrated aggression, but Luke valued subtlety. He understood that discretion could be as powerful as daring. Choosing a safe layup instead of a risky drive was not timidity but wisdom, a recognition that the game rewarded those who thought two shots ahead. This strategic patience reflected his respect for golf's deeper rhythm. It was a game not of force but of flow, where victory often belonged to those who understood when to advance and when to yield. His ability to adapt strategy to context made him unpredictable, frustrating opponents who relied on patterns or assumptions.

The emotional architecture of his play revealed a rare equilibrium. He carried himself with quiet dignity, resisting the theatrical outbursts that often characterized competitive sport. This composure did not imply detachment; it was discipline refined into grace. His focus was internal, anchored by purpose rather than performance anxiety. Spectators who followed his rounds often felt a sense of calm radiating from him, as though his presence steadied the atmosphere around him. That energy spoke to the deeper artistry of temperament, the ability to shape the mood of competition through emotional intelligence.

His sense of aesthetics extended beyond his swing into his entire philosophy of living. Luke often spoke about finding harmony between sport and personal life. He viewed both through the same lens of balance, discipline, and appreciation for detail. The same patience that guided his practice sessions informed his relationships and daily routines. He found beauty in structure, believing that order created space for creativity. This holistic understanding of art and life made him not just a golfer, but a craftsman of experience, someone who sought excellence without sacrificing authenticity.

The contrast between his methodical demeanor and the explosive nature of modern golf invited debate among fans and analysts. Some questioned whether his elegant style could thrive against the growing dominance of raw power. Yet time and again, his results silenced doubts. He demonstrated that accuracy and imagination could compete with distance. His victories reaffirmed that golf remained a game of intellect as much as strength. His approach represented an enduring truth: artistry endures beyond trends, because it touches something universal: the pursuit of perfection through thoughtful creation.

Throughout his career, Luke became an advocate for preserving golf's traditional virtues. He believed that respect for the game's heritage was essential to its soul. He admired players who carried themselves with humility, who treated every round as both privilege and challenge. His speeches at events and interviews often reflected this reverence. To him, golf was not a spectacle to dominate but a dialogue to honor. That ethos shaped how he interacted with fans, opponents, and the media measured, articulate, grounded in respect. His grace under scrutiny became as iconic as his swing.

Artistry, for Luke, was also about adaptation. He recognized that mastery required evolution. Changes in equipment, course design, and competitive culture demanded flexibility without compromise. When his physical game faced challenges whether through injury or the passage of time he responded not with frustration but curiosity. He treated transition as another canvas for exploration. Adjusting technique, refining practice routines, and rethinking course strategy became opportunities to rediscover his craft from new angles. That resilience revealed the artist's mindset: creation thrives through renewal.

Mentorship naturally followed his evolution. Younger players often sought his guidance, drawn to his calm intellect and refined sense of the game. He shared insights not through grand declarations but through examples. Observing his preparation, his course management, his quiet interactions with caddies, offered lessons in professionalism. He emphasized that artistry was built on discipline and that elegance on the course was born from hours of unglamorous work. His mentorship embodied the principle that teaching is an extension of artistry, the passing on of knowledge as an act of creation itself.

The relationship between art and competition often seems paradoxical, yet Luke bridged that divide. His artistry did not diminish his competitiveness; it enhanced it. Beauty and effectiveness coexisted in his approach. The satisfaction of executing a perfectly struck iron or holding a precise put under pressure held aesthetic pleasure as well as strategic success. That fusion of form and function embodied the spirit of golf as both sport and art. Every performance became an exhibition of control shaped by emotion, a balance few achieve with such consistency.

Even off the course, his aesthetic sensibility found expression. Luke had a passion for design, visual art, and music. These interests complemented his sporting identity, reinforcing his sensitivity to detail and proportion. Whether curating spaces, studying architecture, or supporting cultural events, he saw parallels between creative disciplines. Composition, balance, and rhythm connected them all. His appreciation for artistry outside sport enriched his perspective within it, reminding him that golf, too, was an act of creation unfolding in real time.

The public often associated Luke's demeanor with calm, but beneath that tranquility existed the intensity of an artist's fire directed inward. He demanded perfection not from vanity but from devotion to craft. Missed shots haunted him not for their consequences but for their disruption of harmony. He analyzed mistakes not emotionally but analytically, searching for lessons hidden within imperfection. That relentless introspection defined his evolution as both player and artist, revealing that beauty in golf, as in life, often emerges from the discipline to refine imperfection.

Critics sometimes misunderstood his quiet style as lacking aggression. Yet those who knew him best recognized that his calm masked formidable determination. His pursuit of excellence was absolute, though never ostentatious. He approached challenges with the patience of a craftsman shaping stone, deliberate, unhurried, yet unyielding. That quiet tenacity became his greatest strength, a force as enduring as any physical advantage. His art lay in subtlety, his power in precision.

The modern landscape of golf continued to evolve around him, but Luke's artistry retained timeless resonance. His philosophy appealed to purists who valued the game's cerebral and aesthetic dimensions. Younger players studying his technique discovered that restraint could coexist with ambition, that control could amplify confidence. His career stood as living proof that the artistry of golf, its elegance, complexity, and emotional depth remained as relevant as ever, even amid changing styles and technologies.

What distinguished his artistry most profoundly was its emotional authenticity. Every motion reflected not performance but truth. He played with a sincerity that audiences could feel, even if they could not articulate it. Watching him compete evoked calm admiration rather than spectacle-driven excitement. His presence reminded spectators that golf's essence lay not in noise but in silence, the breath held before impact, the echo of a perfect shot disappearing into open air. That quiet poetry defined his legacy.

The art of the game, through Luke Donald's lens, revealed that mastery was not about dominance but understanding of oneself, of nature, of the delicate relationship between effort and grace. He transformed golf into a language of balance and clarity, where beauty and discipline intertwined. Every round became a meditation on control and creativity, every triumph a reminder that true greatness whispers rather than shouts.

His journey illuminated the deeper purpose of sport: to reflect the human spirit's capacity for refinement, patience, and creation. Through him, golf reclaimed its poetic heart, a reminder that the swing of a club could express as much emotion and intellect as any brushstroke or symphony. Luke Donald did not just play the game; he shaped it into art, and through that art, he left an imprint that time cannot erase.

Chapter 8: Challenges, Injuries, and Comebacks

Every athlete who reaches the summit of their sport must, at some point, confront the shadows that accompany greatness. For Luke Donald, the climb had always been marked by meticulous preparation, quiet confidence, and the pursuit of flawless execution. Yet no matter how refined his craft became, no one could insulate themselves completely from the unpredictable nature of sport, the physical strains, the mental turbulence, and the invisible battles that test conviction. His journey through adversity revealed not just the strength of his technique, but the depth of his humanity. Where triumph had defined his rise, resilience would come to define his longevity.

When the first signs of physical strain began to surface, they did not arrive as dramatic breakdowns but as whispers of subtle discomforts in the wrist, back, and neck that seemed manageable at first. Like most professionals, Luke dismissed them as temporary obstacles that could be resolved through rest and therapy. Yet the demands of elite golf rarely grant rest without cost. The repetition of thousands of swings, the hours of travel, and the pressure of maintaining form under scrutiny slowly carved their toll. Pain crept into routine, altering small movements, affecting timing, disturbing rhythm. For a player whose game relied on precision rather than raw power, even the slightest physical imbalance carried profound consequences.

The first real disruption came during seasons when his schedule seemed relentless, his body protesting through fatigue. He pushed through it, believing that discipline and persistence could overcome discomfort. But golf punishes denial as harshly as neglect. Shots that once felt effortless began to betray uncertainty. Timing faltered. Confidence wavered. For someone whose game thrived on rhythm, the erosion of trust in his own motion felt deeply personal. He had built his career on control, and now control itself appeared to be slipping away.

Recovery from physical setbacks required more than medical intervention; it demanded patience that tested his competitive instincts. Rehabilitation sessions replaced tournament rounds. Hours once spent on practice greens became spent in physical therapy rooms, surrounded by resistance bands, heat packs, and careful monitoring. Each stretch, each exercise, carried both frustration and hope. His natural discipline proved an asset here; he treated recovery with the same devotion as training. Yet beneath the professionalism lay emotional fatigue. Watching peers compete while his body resisted cooperation was a quiet torment. He understood that absence from the course meant not just missed opportunities but lost momentum.

When injuries lingered longer than expected, self-doubt began to surface not in loud, dramatic crises, but in quiet reflections during solitary evenings. Questions emerged: had he reached his physical limits? Could the precision that defined his game ever return to its peak? For a player known for serenity, these internal storms were unfamiliar. But rather than surrender to frustration, he sought to understand them. He began studying sports psychology, exploring the link between mental clarity and recovery. The mind, he realized, could either hinder healing or accelerate it. This understanding deepened his awareness of the intricate bond between emotion and performance.

The rehabilitation process became a kind of education. He learned to listen to his body with greater empathy, to respect pain not as an enemy but as communication. He adjusted his swing mechanics to reduce strain, embracing technical changes that once would have felt foreign. Those modifications required courage. Every alteration threatened to disturb habits that had taken decades to build. Yet his analytical nature guided him through it. He treated adaptation not as compromise but as evolution. Each adjustment became an act of creativity, a reconstruction of identity within the framework of survival.

Beyond the physical, the psychological challenges of comeback tested endurance of spirit. Returning to competition after absence meant facing both external skepticism and internal comparison. Fans and analysts had long memories of his peak years, and expectations carried weight. Each round upon return became a measurement not only of score but of restoration of whether the artistry and sharpness that once defined him could resurface. The pressure to prove oneself anew, even to those who once believed, can be heavier than the pressure to succeed for the first time.

He faced stretches where results refused to align with effort. The frustration of missed cuts, close calls, and near-perfect rounds derailed by a single misjudgment accumulated like invisible bruises. Yet those disappointments revealed something deeper about his character. He refused to allow struggle to distort his professionalism. His demeanor remained poised, his respect for the game intact. Reporters noted that even during his lowest rankings, he never abandoned grace. That composure was not resignation, it was resilience disguised as calm.

The physical toll of competition is often intertwined with emotional weariness. Life on tour, once invigorating, could feel isolating when victories seemed distant. Loneliness between tournaments, time spent away from family, and constant comparison to younger competitors compounded the sense of disconnection. Luke, however, discovered strength through perspective. He began focusing on gratitude for the opportunity to compete, for the lessons hidden in hardship, for the enduring support of those closest to him. Gratitude did not erase pain, but it softened its sharpest edges.

His team played a crucial role during these difficult periods. Coaches, trainers, and family formed a network of unwavering belief. His wife and children grounded him, reminding him that identity extended beyond performance. Their encouragement provided emotional stability during moments when confidence faltered. He often described family as his anchor, the quiet force that restored balance when the professional world felt volatile. Those relationships offered not escape but renewal, a reminder that resilience grows strongest in connection.

As his body healed gradually, Luke began to rediscover fragments of his old rhythm. Practice sessions regained fluidity, and confidence, once fragile, started to rebuild. Yet the comeback was never linear. Progress alternated with setbacks, days of precision followed by inexplicable inconsistency. This unpredictability became its own teacher. He learned to detach results from self-worth, focusing instead on process. That shift transformed his outlook. Success ceased to be measured solely by trophies and rankings; it became about mastery of self.

The physical reconstruction of his game paralleled a deeper transformation within. The adversity forced him to reevaluate motivation. Earlier in his career, ambition had driven him toward achievement; now, purpose guided him toward meaning. He no longer sought validation from numbers but fulfillment from the act of competing with authenticity. That maturity infused his performances with a renewed sense of freedom. He played not to reclaim the past, but to redefine what excellence could mean in the present.

Each return to the course carried symbolic weight. The sound of a club meeting ball, the feel of turf beneath his feet, reignited something elemental. Golf, once a battlefield, became again a conversation between memory and renewal, struggle and persistence. Crowds that once expected dominance now offered admiration for endurance. His story had evolved from one of precision to one of perseverance. Fans found inspiration not in his victories alone but in his refusal to abandon the pursuit, even when outcomes seemed uncertain.

The comeback trail exposed the delicate intersection of aging and adaptation. Physical recovery was no longer simply about healing; it was about reinvention. Training routines evolved to emphasize efficiency over intensity. Nutrition, rest, and recovery gained equal importance to practice. He consulted specialists to tailor conditioning specifically for sustainability. Every movement was designed for longevity, not just immediate performance. This pragmatic approach reflected his maturity as a craftsman adjusting tools rather than resisting change.

The mental evolution proved just as significant. He began incorporating meditation and visualization into daily routines, cultivating mindfulness as armor against frustration. The clarity that emerged allowed him to compete with composure, even when results fluctuated. The awareness that his best golf might look different than before did not diminish drive; it redirected it. He embraced the challenge of redefining excellence within his current capabilities. That acceptance liberated him from nostalgia, allowing him to find joy in the present tense of competition.

Critics who once measured him by world rankings began to recognize the depth of his reinvention. Commentators noted the refined balance in his demeanor, the absence of desperation, replaced by quiet assurance. Younger players admired his resilience, drawing lessons from his perseverance through setbacks. His story became an example of how longevity in sport depends not only on physical maintenance but on the ability to evolve emotionally and philosophically.

The process of recovery also expanded his empathy toward others in sport. Experiencing vulnerability made him more attuned to the struggles hidden behind competitors' composed exteriors. He spoke openly about mental health, about the pressures that accompany elite performance, about the need for balance. His candor resonated deeply within the golfing community. He showed that resilience is not stoicism but the courage to confront fragility without shame. This honesty strengthened his bond with fans who saw their own struggles reflected in his transparency.

There were moments of resurgence that reignited belief. A string of strong finishes, flashes of the touch that once ruled the greens, reminded the world of his brilliance. Each success felt richer because it was earned through struggle. The satisfaction was not about proving doubters wrong but about proving endurance right. Every competitive round became a testament to persistence, a quiet declaration that artistry and resolve could coexist with time's inevitable changes.

Off the course, these experiences reshaped his outlook on mentorship and leadership. He became more deliberate in guiding younger golfers, not merely on technique but on navigating the psychological labyrinth of professional life. His advice emphasized patience, humility, and the understanding that setbacks do not erase talent but refine it. His journey had taught him that greatness is not defined by an uninterrupted rise but by the ability to rebuild oneself after falling.

The concept of comeback, for Luke Donald, transcended mere return to form. It symbolized transformation, a shift from striving for perfection to embracing imperfection with purpose. Injuries had stripped him of certain physical advantages, but they had gifted him perspective. They taught him to value process over outcome, resilience over results, meaning over metrics. This philosophical clarity turned pain into teacher, loss into catalyst.

The arc of his later years on tour reflected this rebirth. While victories became rarer, his performances carried depth and emotional resonance. Each tournament represented gratitude for endurance rather than pursuit of dominance. His swing, though subtly altered, retained elegance. The grace that once defined his artistry now blended with the wisdom of survival. Watching him play became an experience not of nostalgia but admiration for a man who had weathered storms and still found beauty in the struggle.

Adversity also refined his understanding of legacy. He came to realize that what endures beyond trophies are the lessons one leaves behind the embodiment of professionalism, humility, and perseverance. His comeback was less about reclaiming status and more about demonstrating that excellence evolves with time. Through his resilience, he redefined what success meant: not the absence of pain, but the strength to continue through it.

His story resonates because it mirrors the universal human journey: the confrontation with limitation, the necessity of adaptation, the rediscovery of purpose after loss. Fans who once admired him for precision now revered him for courage. Fellow professionals, regardless of generation, found inspiration in his ability to maintain grace amid uncertainty. His career became not only a testament to skill but to spirit proof that even the most refined art must sometimes be remade through hardship.

The narrative of Luke Donald's challenges, injuries, and comebacks encapsulates the essence of endurance. It reveals the truth that greatness is not preserved in the absence of struggle but shaped by it. Through the pain of physical strain, the doubt of decline, and the humility of recovery, he crafted a new form of excellence one measured not by dominance but by dignity. His journey stands as a reminder that even when the body falters, the will to rise can turn survival into something profoundly beautiful.

Luke Donald's resilience illuminated the deeper meaning of sport: that the true victory lies not in perfect performance, but in the courage to rebuild when perfection fades. His comebacks were not returns to what once was, but progressions toward what could still be a living portrait of endurance painted in patience, intelligence, and unbreakable grace. Through those chapters of struggle, he revealed the art of renewal, and in doing so, carved his place not only among champions, but among those who remind the world that greatness endures through perseverance.

CHAPTER 9: CAPTAINCY AND LEGACY

Luke Donald's appointment as captain of Team Europe for the Ryder Cup represented a moment of both destiny and responsibility. His career had been a model of quiet achievement, but leadership at this scale required something more a synthesis of experience, character, and vision. When he was handed the reins, the golfing world viewed him not as the loudest or most flamboyant choice, but as the most intelligent and balanced. The role demanded calm under pressure, strategic depth, emotional insight, and the ability to unite a group of athletes with distinct personalities into one cohesive force. Donald's life and career had prepared him perfectly for this kind of challenge.

The Ryder Cup, unlike any other tournament, tests more than technical ability. It is a contest of pride, identity, and endurance, a stage where individual stars must set aside ego for the collective cause. For

Luke, who had always valued precision, discipline, and teamwork, the captaincy was an opportunity to lead through authenticity. He understood the pulse of the competition, having lived through its fierce rivalries and experienced both its elation and heartbreak. He had been one of Europe's most reliable performers, often quietly delivering crucial points without seeking the spotlight. That humility made him relatable to players and credible as a leader. His approach was rooted in meticulous preparation and empathy.

His first steps as captain were deliberate. He focused on building relationships, not hierarchies. Instead of dictating roles, he sought conversations with each player, trying to understand their state of mind, motivations, and comfort zones. His method was psychological as much as strategic. He believed that confidence on the course came from trusting it. To Donald, leadership was about creating an atmosphere where everyone felt valued and secure, regardless of ranking or reputation. He wanted each member of the team to feel a sense of belonging and belief. That sense of collective identity had been a hallmark of Europe's past successes, and he aimed to revive it.

Preparation became an art form. Donald immersed himself in analytics, course data, and historical performance trends. He was not a leader who relied on instinct alone; his decisions were supported by layers of research. He examined player pairings, compatibility based on temperament and playing style, and past success rates under different conditions. His attention to detail extended to travel schedules, rest routines, and even practice tempos. Every aspect of the week was orchestrated to ensure players could perform at their psychological and physical peak. He treated the captaincy as a craft, just as he had treated his own golf swing as something to be studied, refined, and perfected.

Donald's leadership was also grounded in emotion. He knew the Ryder Cup was as much about passion as precision. He made it a priority to connect the team's mission with heritage. He reminded his players of what the tournament symbolized: the unity of Europe, the pride of representing generations of golfers, and the shared memories of those who had lifted the cup before them. He invited past legends to speak, not to lecture, but to inspire. He wanted his players to feel part of a lineage rather than just a team assembled for a single event. That sense of continuity became a quiet source of strength.

During practice sessions, Donald's composure radiated through the camp. He never raised his voice, never panicked, and never allowed tension to dominate the environment. His calm confidence became contagious. Players spoke about how his demeanor made them feel steady, even under immense pressure. His feedback was specific and constructive, focused on solutions rather than problems. He was a leader who noticed the smallest details: the angle of a stance, the rhythm of a swing, or a flicker of doubt in a player's eyes. He would address it with tact, often through subtle conversation rather than overt critique.

When the matches began, his planning came to life. Every pairing seemed carefully chosen to balance personalities and styles. Some partnerships were intuitive, others unexpected, but each was based on compatibility rather than reputation. Donald's approach was to maximize synergy. He valued chemistry over hierarchy, believing that emotional connection between teammates could elevate their performance beyond the sum of their parts. He positioned his players not just according to skill, but to mindset, placing the right temperament in the right moments.

His communication throughout the event was measured and precise. He knew that leadership during the Ryder Cup required more listening than talking. Players often described how he gave them space to express their own instincts while providing quiet guidance. He had a knack for saying exactly what needed to be said, no more and no less. Whether it was a short phrase of encouragement before a tee shot or a subtle nod after a missed putt, his presence was steady and reassuring. That understated authority became his hallmark.

Donald's success as captain revealed how much the sport had evolved. Golf, traditionally an individual pursuit, required a new kind of leadership in the team format, one that blended emotional intelligence with modern data analysis. Luke embodied both. He treated the Ryder Cup as a living ecosystem where analytics met human emotion. He didn't rely solely on numbers; he balanced them with intuition born of years of experience. His decisions reflected a blend of science and art, logic and empathy, a combination that few could match.

His leadership extended beyond tactics. He paid close attention to culture, ensuring that team chemistry remained genuine. He encouraged laughter during meals, relaxed interactions during downtime, and open dialogue during strategy sessions. His belief was simple: a relaxed mind performs better than a tense one. He fostered an atmosphere where players could be themselves, where camaraderie replaced anxiety, and where competition was viewed as a shared journey rather than an individual burden.

Observers noted how the European camp under Donald had an air of calm determination. There was no bravado, no loud declarations, just quiet conviction. He allowed the players to own their roles, to feel empowered rather than controlled. His leadership style drew parallels to conductors of orchestras guiding, not dominating, allowing each musician to play their part while ensuring harmony across the performance. That was the essence of Luke Donald's captaincy: structure without rigidity, passion without chaos, belief without arrogance.

When victory came, it was not just a triumph of skill but of unity. Players spoke of how Donald's presence had given them clarity. He had managed to create an atmosphere where every player felt both individually significant and collectively responsible. His humility set the tone; no one was above the team, not even the captain himself. His post-match words reflected gratitude rather than self-congratulation. He credited the players, the support staff, and the fans, reinforcing the sense that the win belonged to everyone.

His captaincy also became a study in modern sports leadership. Analysts and commentators pointed out that his methods mirrored corporate and psychological best practices: communication rooted in empathy, preparation guided by data, and culture built on trust. His approach demonstrated that leadership in sport had transcended the old model of command-and-control. It had evolved into collaboration, emotional intelligence, and shared vision. Luke Donald became an example not only for golf but for leadership beyond sport.

The legacy of his captaincy reached deeper than trophies. For the younger generation of golfers, he became a mentor who embodied grace and resilience. He showed that greatness in golf was not just about power or charisma, but about consistency, thoughtfulness, and respect. He had lived through eras dominated by flamboyant personalities, yet his own success reaffirmed that quiet strength could be equally magnetic. His journey from a technical craftsman on the fairways to a respected leader symbolized the full circle of an athlete's life.

His leadership also carried symbolic meaning for European golf. He represented a bridge between eras connecting the disciplined traditions of past captains with the analytical precision of modern sport. He respected heritage while embracing innovation. Under his watch, Europe's team culture adapted to the evolving realities of global golf without losing its essence. He blended the old spirit of camaraderie with the new language of performance science.

Beyond the matches, Donald's influence continued through mentoring and commentary. Younger players often sought his advice on course management, composure, and mental conditioning. He shared insights not as lectures but as reflections, always encouraging others to develop their own identities rather than mimic his. His humility made his advice resonate. He believed that authenticity was the key to longevity, a principle that had guided his own career.

As years passed, discussions of his legacy grew. Writers and analysts often described him as one of the sport's great thinkers, not just a player of skill, but a strategist of substance. His calm presence, thoughtful communication, and meticulous planning became case studies for future leaders. His legacy was not built on dramatic speeches or iconic moments but on a sustained demonstration of integrity and intelligence. He proved that leadership could be quiet yet profoundly powerful.

His captaincy also shaped perceptions of European golf's identity on the global stage. It reaffirmed that the continent's success was rooted not only in talent but in collective spirit. Under his guidance, the European team reminded the world that collaboration, respect, and belief could overcome individual brilliance. His influence reached beyond the scoreboard, helping preserve the cultural DNA of European golf amid a rapidly commercialized era.

Luke Donald's journey from player to captain encapsulated the evolution of an athlete into a statesman. His leadership reflected not only his character but the lessons of a lifetime of patience, preparation, and grace under pressure. Every decision, every gesture, carried the weight of his values. His ability to remain calm when others grew anxious, to see patterns when others saw chaos, defined his leadership as much as it had defined his playing career. He became the embodiment of balance, the fusion of mind and heart, analysis and instinct.

His legacy will endure not because of a single victory but because of the culture he strengthened. He reminded golf that respect and excellence are not opposing forces but partners. His story continues to inspire future captains, players, and leaders who see in him a model of how to lead with quiet authority and emotional intelligence. His legacy is not measured solely by wins but by the integrity he carried through every phase of his journey.

Luke Donald's captaincy confirmed what many had sensed throughout his playing days that he was never just a golfer; he was an artist of leadership. He conducted the Ryder Cup as he had conducted his own career: with precision, depth, and a rare understanding of human connection. His impact will echo across generations, a reminder that greatness is not always loud; sometimes, it is the calm voice that brings others together and turns a group of talented individuals into a team that believes. His chapter as captain closed with dignity, but its resonance remains, shaping the spirit of golf across continents and generations.

CHAPTER 10: BEYOND THE FAIRWAYS

When the noise of the tournaments fades and the applause settles into memory, a different rhythm begins to define a sportsman's life. For Luke Donald, that rhythm was never abrupt or disorienting. His career had always been built on patience and reflection, and those qualities naturally extended into his world beyond the fairways. His post-competitive years were not a retreat from relevance but a quiet evolution into a more expansive form of purpose. The golf course had been his stage, but the lessons drawn from its challenges became the foundation of a more rounded and meaningful life.

His transition from the intensity of competition to a more balanced existence was seamless because he had always approached life with equilibrium. Even at the height of his playing career, he was known for his composure and self-awareness. When that phase gave way to new pursuits, he viewed it not as an ending but as an opportunity to apply his discipline and creativity to different arenas. He understood that his reputation extended beyond the scorecards. He carried the responsibility of being an ambassador for golf and a model for professionalism. That awareness shaped his activities and relationships in the years after full-time play.

Family became his anchor. His devotion to his wife and children reflected the same steadiness that had marked his golf career. The demands of professional sport often pull athletes away from home, but Luke had always tried to maintain presence even amid travel and competition. Once his schedule loosened, he embraced the chance to invest fully in the moments he had once only glimpsed between tournaments. School events, family trips, shared meals these became treasures he cherished with the same intensity he had once reserved for major championships. The small, quiet rituals of domestic life grounded him. He often spoke about how his family's support had been the unseen force behind his achievements, and now it was his turn to offer that support back.

The discipline that once governed his practice sessions found expression in his dedication to mentorship. Young players often approached him not for technical advice but for perspective on how to manage pressure, how to balance ambition with wellbeing, and how to maintain composure when success feels distant. Luke offered guidance that reflected the emotional intelligence he had developed over decades of competition. He understood that the mental game was often more decisive than the physical one. He emphasized self-knowledge, patience, and process over results. To him, greatness was not about perfection but about resilience and growth. Those conversations often left a deep impression on rising golfers who admired his humility and depth.

Beyond direct mentorship, Donald engaged with the sport through commentary, consultancy, and developmental programs. He viewed golf not just as a competition but as a craft capable of shaping character. His initiatives often centered on youth programs designed to expand access to the sport and promote values such as integrity and respect. He wanted golf to be a vehicle for education, teaching young players not only how to strike a ball but how to carry themselves. His own experience from modest beginnings to global recognition made him a credible advocate for perseverance. He saw potential in every aspiring player who was willing to learn, regardless of their background.

Off the course, Luke's passion for art became a defining part of his identity. Long before his name was associated with trophies, he had studied art at university, and that interest never left him. The relationship between art and golf had always been intimate for him both required patience, rhythm, and sensitivity to form. Over time, he began to collect art, not as a display of wealth but as a dialogue with creativity. His taste leaned toward modern and abstract works that emphasized precision and balance, qualities he valued in his own pursuits. Art offered him a language to express thoughts that competition never allowed space for. It became both a hobby and a reflection of his inner life.

He often described painting and sculpture as parallel disciplines to the swing. Both demanded harmony between control and release. Both celebrated individuality within structure. The galleries and studios he visited became sanctuaries where he could engage with beauty stripped of competition. He also developed friendships within the art world, finding inspiration in conversations with artists whose craft involved as much introspection as performance. This connection between artistic creativity and athletic focus gave his post-playing life a distinct dimension. It illustrated how identity could expand beyond professional boundaries without losing authenticity.

Luke's philanthropic endeavors deepened over time. He had long participated in charity events, but as his calendar opened, he began to shape initiatives more personally. His causes often revolved around children's health, education, and the environment issues that resonated with his values of balance and stewardship. He believed that those who had benefited from opportunity owed it to others to create new ones. His philanthropy reflected the same quiet sincerity that defined his personality. He avoided grandstanding, preferring to work behind the scenes, ensuring that contributions reached tangible outcomes. To him, charity was not a platform but a responsibility.

His public image remained one of integrity. In a sport often associated with ego, he stood apart for his modesty and poise. That reputation followed him into every project he undertook. Corporations and organizations sought his involvement precisely because he embodied trust. His endorsement carried the weight of credibility, not marketing flair. He lent his name only to ventures that aligned with his principles. Whether collaborating on golf course design, sustainability programs, or youth development initiatives, he brought the same meticulous care that had defined his playing style. His influence came not from loud advocacy but from quiet examples.

Retirement also allowed him to reflect on his relationship with time. During his competitive years, every minute had been scheduled, every week organized around tournaments and training. The absence of that rigid structure initially felt strange, but it also opened space for renewal. He learned to appreciate slowness, the unhurried rhythm of a morning walk, the freedom of playing a casual round without scorekeeping, and the joy of reading or sketching for its own sake. He discovered that fulfillment no longer depended on performance. Contentment came from awareness, from being fully present in life's ordinary moments. That mindfulness enriched his relationships and deepened his gratitude for the journey he had lived.

Travel remained part of his life, though its purpose shifted. Instead of airports and competition schedules, his journeys became explorations of culture, art, and human connection. Whether walking through European galleries, visiting communities supported by his foundations, or attending global golf events as an observer, he approached travel with curiosity rather than ambition. He had seen much of the world through the lens of competition; now he wanted to experience it through appreciation. His quiet reflections during these travels often found their way into speeches, interviews, and essays that revealed a contemplative side rarely visible during his playing years.

The legacy he built off the course continued to intertwine with his sporting achievements. People who met him were struck by how seamlessly grace translated into every sphere of his life. His success had never been loud, and his influence after retirement was similarly steady, enduring, and quietly transformative. He became a reference point for what it meant to navigate fame with dignity. Young athletes, executives, and even artists often cited him as an example of how to pursue excellence without losing oneself. His calm demeanor, thoughtful articulation, and unwavering courtesy made him a rare figure in a world often consumed by self-promotion.

He also began to reflect publicly on the philosophy of sport. In lectures and panel discussions, he explored how competition could coexist with artistry, how structure could nurture freedom, and how athletes could sustain emotional health in high-pressure environments. His reflections drew from personal experience from the days of striving for perfection to the lessons learned through setbacks and renewal. He spoke of how failure could serve as a teacher, how patience often outlasted power, and how meaning in sport came not from dominance but from connection to one's craft, teammates, and audience. His words resonated because they were grounded in authenticity rather than rhetoric.

Golf course architecture became another avenue through which Luke expressed his sensibilities. His approach to design mirrored his playing philosophy subtle, intelligent, and respectful of natural landscapes. He worked with design teams to create layouts that emphasized strategic thought over brute strength. His goal was to build courses that rewarded creativity and precision, values that had defined his own career. He often said that a great course should tell a story, inviting players to think, adapt, and feel. This pursuit allowed him to merge his love of art, nature, and golf into one enduring legacy. Each design carried traces of his personality, balance, elegance, and thoughtfulness.

As time went on, his role as a public figure evolved into that of a statesman for the sport. When he spoke, people listened not because he was the loudest voice, but because his words carried depth. He represented a generation of golfers who valued substance over spectacle. His perspective bridged eras; he understood the traditions of the game while recognizing its modern challenges. Whether addressing issues of sportsmanship, sustainability, or inclusivity, he advocated with quiet conviction. He believed golf should remain both a competitive sport and a humanizing experience, accessible yet aspirational.

His relationship with fans endured, marked by mutual respect. People admired not just what he achieved but how he conducted himself through victory and adversity. His demeanor remained unchanged, approachable, thoughtful, and gracious. Even years after stepping away from regular competition, galleries and autograph lines greeted him with warmth that reflected genuine affection. He represented something timeless: the idea that true greatness lies not only in talent but in character.

As he aged, reflection became a larger part of his daily rhythm. The trophies on his shelves were reminders of moments past, but they did not define his sense of fulfillment. What mattered more were the relationships, lessons, and memories that shaped his identity. He often spoke about gratitude for the mentors who guided him, the fans who supported him, and the family who stood beside him through every chapter. That sense of appreciation gave his later years a quiet radiance. He had not just succeeded; he had endured with grace.

Luke Donald's life beyond the fairways illustrates the full arc of human growth. He moved from ambition to mastery, from mastery to leadership, and from leadership to wisdom. Each stage added depth rather than replacing the previous one. His story is not only about golf but about the art of living with balance. He demonstrated that the qualities cultivated through sport discipline, awareness, humility can illuminate every domain of life. His legacy is written not only in record books but in the countless individuals inspired by his example.

For those who followed his career, his post-playing journey offered reassurance that purpose does not fade with competition. It evolves. His capacity to adapt, to find beauty in new forms, and to give back to the communities that shaped him reflects a rare wholeness. He remained a maestro, but his orchestra expanded beyond greens and bunkers to include art, mentorship, philanthropy, and reflection. The same steady rhythm that once guided his swing now guided his life deliberate, thoughtful, and quietly brilliant.

Luke Donald's world beyond the fairways stands as a portrait of grace sustained. It reveals how a life built on discipline and humility can continue to create harmony long after the applause fades. His influence lingers wherever excellence meets empathy on the course, in classrooms, in galleries, and within the lives of those who learned from his example. The calm that once steadied his hands over a putt now steadies those who look to him for guidance. His legacy is the quiet assurance that greatness is not a moment but a way of being enduring, generous, and beautifully human.

CONCLUSION

There's something quietly magnetic about Luke Donald's story, the way he moved through the world of golf not as a roaring conqueror but as a man who played with purpose, thought, and artistry. He wasn't the type to pound his chest after a perfect drive or ignite fireworks with wild celebrations. Instead, he brought a rhythm to golf that was closer to poetry than spectacle. Watching him over the years was like watching a master craftsman, someone who believed that greatness wasn't a performance but a process. His legacy now stands not only on leaderboards but in the calm confidence he inspired across generations of athletes and dreamers.

What made Luke's journey captivating was that it never felt manufactured. His personality was disarmingly genuine, his smile unforced, his voice always steady. He wasn't the type to demand attention, yet he inevitably commanded it. People leaned in when he spoke, not because he shouted, but because he didn't need to. His calm became his charisma. The world of sports often celebrates noise, the flash, the drama, the extremes. Luke reminded everyone that composure could be just as compelling. His story is proof that quiet determination, when combined with precision and imagination, can move mountains or in his case, golf balls that refuse to miss their mark.

There's also something deeply relatable about his path. He wasn't the prodigy who burst onto the scene with reckless dominance. He built his success one stroke at a time, through repetition, reflection, and resilience. That's why so many people saw themselves in him. He represented the idea that mastery isn't about talent alone, it's about patience, humility, and the courage to evolve. When he was chasing perfection, he never sacrificed integrity for glory. When he faced setbacks, he didn't collapse;

he recalibrated. It's the kind of approach that resonates far beyond golf. Anyone who's ever tried to achieve something meaningful knows the rhythm of Luke's story: steady work, silent growth, and the long, rewarding pursuit of balance.

Part of his charm came from how effortlessly he blended grace with grit. On the surface, his calm demeanor made everything look easy, but underneath that composure lived a relentless competitor. He didn't need to raise his voice to make a statement; his play did that for him. There was steel behind his softness, a reminder that gentleness and strength are not opposites but companions. His ability to hold both qualities at once made him stand apart from the louder narratives of his era. He never needed chaos to prove passion. His version of intensity was quieter but just as fierce, rooted in focus rather than frenzy.

Beyond the trophies and accolades, what continues to shine about Luke Donald is his sense of identity. He knew who he was, both on and off the course, and that consistency became his signature. Whether addressing a press conference, mentoring a young golfer, or walking down the fairway under pressure, he carried himself with a kind of timeless class. He didn't chase trends or bend to expectations. His authenticity was magnetic precisely because it was effortless. In an age obsessed with reinvention, Luke reminded the world that being true to oneself is the most powerful form of style.

It's also impossible to talk about his legacy without mentioning how beautifully human his career felt. There were moments of triumph that seemed transcendent, but there were also slumps, injuries, and quiet battles that tested his resolve. Through it all, he never lost perspective. He allowed himself to grow without bitterness, to evolve without ego. That balance between ambition and contentment gave his story emotional depth. He wasn't afraid to admit vulnerability, and that honesty only deepened his appeal. Golf fans respected his skill; people admired his grace under pressure; but those who paid attention loved him for his humility.

His presence off the course enriched the portrait even more. Luke didn't retreat into silence after the peak years he expanded. His creativity flowed into other passions, his leadership inspired younger athletes, and his contributions to the sport's culture became lasting. He turned his artistry into mentorship, his experiences into lessons. His post-playing life was not a quiet retirement but a continuation of the same philosophy that made him great: refine, reflect, and give back. He became living proof that success doesn't end when the competition does. For him, excellence was a lifelong practice, not a momentary achievement.

What truly endears Luke to so many people is that he represents the kind of heroism that feels attainable. He wasn't powered by mythic strength or wild flamboyance; he succeeded through discipline, empathy, and imagination. He showed that thoughtfulness could coexist with competitiveness, that humility could walk hand-in-hand with victory. His life reminds us that there's beauty in precision and power in patience. He taught his fans, his peers, and even casual observers that mastery is not about domination but harmony, a harmony between mind, body, and soul.

Looking back, his journey feels like a meditation on grace. Every chapter from his rise through the ranks to his time leading others speaks to the idea that true greatness is less about noise and more about resonance. He played the game like a composer crafting a symphony, each note deliberate, each pause meaningful. Even in retirement, his legacy continues to hum softly beneath the surface of the sport, influencing players who grew up watching him and fans who still find comfort in his example. He left behind not just memories, but a mindset one that values awareness over aggression, thought over impulse, and integrity over spectacle.

It's refreshing to see how naturally Luke embraced life beyond competition. There's joy in how he continues to approach each day curious, creative, grounded. Whether he's mentoring young athletes, exploring art, or spending time with his family, he carries that same sense of calm mastery. The game may have shaped him, but it didn't define him. That's what separates the truly special figures in sport from the rest: the ability to grow beyond their arena without losing the essence that made them remarkable. Luke Donald is that kind of figure: a man who didn't just play golf; he lived it, understood it, and translated its lessons into the rhythm of his daily life.

His biography, like his career, leaves readers with a quiet sense of inspiration rather than awe. It doesn't shout; it lingers. It reminds us that success built on thoughtfulness has a different kind of power, one that endures longer than fame or flash. Luke's life is proof that you don't have to dominate headlines to make a lasting impact. Sometimes, all it takes is consistency, kindness, and the courage to be authentic in a world that celebrates noise. He gave golf something rare: a soul shaped by both intellect and heart.

If there's one takeaway from his journey, it's that elegance isn't a style, it's a philosophy. Whether holding a club, guiding a team, or walking through life's quieter moments, Luke embodied the art of being deliberate. Every choice, every word, every gesture seemed to come from a place of awareness.

That's why his story continues to resonate long after the scorecards have faded. He turned a solitary sport into a reflection of human creativity, and in doing so, he offered a different kind of heroism, one built on grace, respect, and purpose.

So, if you ever find yourself standing on a course, staring down a fairway, take a page from Luke Donald's story. Breathe. Trust your rhythm. Focus on the moment rather than the noise. The ball doesn't have to be crushed; it just needs to be placed with intention. That philosophy, simple but profound, extends far beyond sport. It's about finding balance in chaos, calm in motion, and beauty in restraint. That's what Luke Donald gave to golf and to anyone who's ever strived to master their craft with dignity and heart.

And perhaps that's the magic of it all: Luke Donald made excellence feel human. He showed that a steady hand, a kind spirit, and a thoughtful mind could still shape legends. His story reminds us that being extraordinary isn't about being the loudest or the boldest, it's about being true to yourself, no matter the stage. The fairways may fade into memory, but the man who walked them with such quiet brilliance will remain an enduring symbol of what it means to be a maestro not just of golf, but of life itself.

Printed in Dunstable, United Kingdom